JOHN WESLEY'S

SUNDAY SERVICE

OF THE

METHODISTS

IN

NORTH AMERICA

with an introduction by James F. White

Quarterly Review

John Wesley's Sunday Service of the Methodists in North America
with an Introduction by James F. White
Methodist Bicentennial Commemorative Reprint

ISBN 0-687-40632-3

CONTENTS

The Sunday Service

For Susan

PREFACE

John Wesley's *Sunday Service of the Methodists in North America* is, in a sense, the last will and testament of the octogenarian patriarch of Methodism to his American followers. At the same time, the book is the foundation stone for subsequent Methodist worship in this country. Until the 1970s, material from the *Sunday Service* was American Methodism's chief link to the worship of the ancient Church, the funnel through which the whole history of Christian worship poured into local churches. Thus it is a pivotal document linking American Methodist worship to that of the Church Universal by way of the Anglican tradition.

In the years since the Second Vatican Council, broader contacts with the worship life of other Christians have reached American Methodism. Documents from the early Church, unknown to Wesley and his contemporaries, have reshaped the worship of the churches of the West. Hand in hand have come new developments in biblical and historical scholarship and in liturgical theology. In The United Methodist Church, the impact of such broader contacts with universal Christianity, in both its ancient and modern forms, is apparent in each volume of the Supplemental Worship Resources series. These volumes reveal a breadth of scope impossible in Wesley's time, but one which he, almost certainly, would have welcomed warmly.

In the midst of the new reformation in word and sacrament of our times, it is vital in order to deepen and sustain such reforming that the people called Methodists keep contact with their own historical roots. And it is clear that any understanding of what is distinctive in Methodist worship must begin with Wesley's legacy. The *Sunday Service* is the heart of his bequest and manifests his intentions most explicitly. Unfortunately, of the two thousand copies of the *Sunday Service* printed in 1784 for

7

shipment to America, only approximately thirty-eight survive, and these are seen by few. This facsimile edition is intended to resolve that difficulty by making it possible for many to have access to an exact reproduction of one of the rare originals. This reproduction should be an important asset in commemoration of the bicentennial of American Methodism's independent existence.

In this edition, a 1784 copy of the *Sunday Service* has been reproduced in full with the exceptions of the collects, epistles, and gospel (which are still in use and available in a current English *Book of Common Prayer*) and the Psalter (likewise accessible, although without Wesley's emendations). An introduction has been added to provide general information about the book. The notes highlight other specific matters, such as the significant changes that Wesley made from the BCP, and indicate many of his precedents. The prayer book used for comparison has been an edition published in Oxford in 1784. It was "Printed by W. Jackson and A. Hamilton, Printers to the University" and contains all the services Wesley used.

Thanks are due to Dr. Kenneth E. Rowe of Drew University Library for making available the copies used for reproduction from Drew's magnificent collection of Methodistica and for his continuing gracious help during my research. The courtesies of other librarians at Seabury-Western Theological Seminary, Pierpont Morgan Library, Union Theological Seminary, United Methodist Publishing House, Candler School of Theology, Boston University School of Theology, General Theological Seminary, and Perkins School of Theology have enabled me to inspect personally sixteen of the surviving copies of the 1784 edition. Professors A. Raymond George, Frank Baker, and Richard P. Heitzenrater have read the manuscript and contributed from their great stores of learning. E. Farley Sharp has devoted much patient expertise in producing clear reproductions from often unclear originals. I am greatly indebted to my wife, Susan J. White, for constant assistance at every stage during my research and writing. I dedicate this work to her with gratitude.

JAMES F. WHITE
University of Notre Dame
March 11, 1983

INTRODUCTION

John Wesley's *Sunday Service* is, as its name indicates, a service book rather than a prayer book. It is intended to be used on the Lord's Day for public worship; only the litany is directed to be read on other days ("on Wednesdays and Fridays") and prayer is to be "extempore on all other days." Except for Christmas Day, Good Friday, and Ascension Day, no provision is made for weekday use, and the occasional services occur only as needed. The only exception to the sole use on Sunday in public worship is the provision of an abbreviated Psalter. This is structured for morning and evening prayer readings over a thirty-day period, but with no further instructions about its intended use. We may presume that the Psalter was to be used in private with daily extempore prayer. But the Psalter has been censored of psalms and verses "highly improper for the mouths of a Christian Congregation," a phrase which suggests that it is intended for weekly corporate use rather than in daily private devotions.

Wesley's effort to provide worship forms for "those poor sheep in the wilderness" takes into account the radically different situation in the "States," where English civil and ecclesiastical authority had vanished "by a very uncommon train of providences." Wesley prunes away all the paraphernalia of an established national church. He resolves the uncertainty (in 1784) as to the leaders of civil government in America with ambiguous prayers for "the Supreme Rulers of these United States."

Wesley recognized that social conditions, too, were radically different. His book was intended for itinerant preachers in the process of gathering congregations rather than for established clergy in parish churches. Although Wesley's services follow formal structures from the *Book of Common Prayer* (BCP hereafter), his *Sunday Service* adds provision for the elder to "put up an Extempore Prayer" at the eucharist, and his letter suggests the same for weekday prayer. The absence of any choral bodies in American Methodism is acknowledged in changing all rubrics which read: "Then shall be said or sung" to "Then shall be said." Service music has been removed, although abundant congregational song in the form of hymnody is presupposed by *A Collection of Psalms and Hymns for the Lord's Day* bound with the *Sunday Service*. Wesley's distaste for anthems as inappropriate for "joint worship" is evident in his act of discarding the rubric: "In Quires and Places where they sing, here followeth the Anthem" from both morning and evening prayer. Hymnody, which Wesley believed accessible to all, has replaced service music and anthems.

Little is presupposed architecturally. Rubrics about the arrangement of liturgical space are usually eliminated except for a few, very few, essential references: "The Elder, kneeling down at the Table," or "The Minister coming to the Font." Many references, but not all, to kneeling are removed. The most surprising remnant of a settled society is the retention of the marriage banns which "must be published in the Congregation, three several Sundays, in the Time of Divine Service" although the term "Congregation" has supplanted "Church." Mention of the church building disappears from the burial of the dead although one rubric suggests procession, probably to the building, while another indicates a different location, "At the Grave." All references to clerical garb are carefully eliminated throughout the *Sunday Service*. In short, a minimum of musical talent and architectural resources are needed for the worship Wesley envisions for North America. Flexibility and adaptability are provided for instead.

Notwithstanding all of Wesley's political, ecclesiastical, and cultural adaptations, his service book is a deeply conservative work, the product of one deeply, though not uncritically, enamored of the BCP. Every page of the *Sunday Service* bears marks, not of a casual reviser, but of one who had read or heard the prayerbook daily throughout eight decades, and who is determined to retain all that wore well and to discard only that which proved inadequate in his own experience. Wesley's Preface indicates his conviction that no ancient or modern liturgy "breathes more of a solid, scriptural, rational Piety than

10

the Common Prayer of the Church of England," and such a feeling is certainly witnessed to by his editing the prayer book for "our Societies in America." Wesley treats the BCP as "our incomparable liturgy" as had Anglicans long before his birth. Thus, if one sets aside the necessary political, ecclesiastical, and cultural changes, it is basically a conservative revision (in some ways more so even than the proposed 1786 BCP of the Protestant Episcopal Church).

Wesley's conservatism is most apparent in the treatment of the Lord's Supper. The 166 eucharistic hymns of the Wesleys allowed considerable enrichment of the doctrines expressed in the Anglican rite, but the rite itself was changed little theologically by Wesley. The *Sunday Service*, then, is basically the work of one who loved the BCP and was determined to preserve it for others by adapting it to their changed circumstances.

I

Certain mysteries remain with regard to the production of Wesley's book from its inception until it was accepted at the "Christmas Conference" of the new Methodist Episcopal Church in Baltimore on December 27, 1784. We may presume that Wesley made his changes in a copy of the prayer book and certainly one, such as the Oxford printing of 1784, that included the ordinal and Articles of Religion. Dr. Thomas Coke saw it through the printer, William Strahan's firm in London. The pages were shipped across the Atlantic unbound in order to avoid the extra duty on bound volumes and was bound in New York. In the process, some alterations were made but it is impossible to pronounce precisely by whom. Five years afterward, in a letter dated June 20, 1789, Wesley wrote that "Dr. Coke made two or three little alterations in the Prayer-Book without my knowledge. I took particular care throughout to alter nothing merely for altering's sake. In religion I am for as few innovations as possible. I love the old wine best. And if it were only on this account, I prefer 'which' before 'who art in heaven.' "[1] Since editions also were published in 1786 and 1788, also with Coke's assistance, it is difficult to be certain that it was Coke who was responsible for the changes in 1784, although it

1. *Letters*, edited by John Telford (London: Epworth Press, 1931), VIII, 144-45.

seems likely. Nor does Wesley recollect, apparently, that he had himself changed the Lord's Prayer at two minor points throughout the book: "which" to "who art" and "in earth" to "on earth."

A mystery in the 1784 printing involves the elimination and restoration of the manual acts in the prayer of consecration at the eucharist and the sign of the cross in the rite of infant baptism. On the basis of the conservatism expressed in Wesley's 1789 letter, it seems most likely that he preferred to retain the manual acts and the sign of the cross, that Coke deleted both, and that Wesley sent along corrected sheets (following his original intentions) with the insistence that they be substituted for the defective pages 135-36 and 141-44 when the books were bound in America.[2] Not all were inserted as intended. Both versions exist today, one with all the original and corrected pages (Pierpont Morgan Library) and another with both sets of pages 135-36 (Pittsburgh Theological Seminary). The manual acts appear in subsequent editions, but the signation disappears, and such has been the situation throughout Methodist history until the 1970s. Variety also exists in the presence or absence of both Wesley's letter to the Methodist clergy in "North-America" of September 10, 1784, and his preface dated the day before.

Adoption by the 1784 Christmas Conference by no means insured widespread use of the *Sunday Service,* although copies were kept in print for American use during Wesley's lifetime. Subsequent editions specifically intended for American use were published in 1786 bearing the subtitle: *In the United States of America* and, in 1790: *In the United-States of America . . . The Fourth Edition.* Other editions appeared in 1788 and 1792, some copies of which were intended for American use. But after the death of Wesley and the 1792 General Conference, the 314-page *Sunday Service* virtually disappeared except for 37 pages of "Sacramental Services &c." and the "Articles of Religion." The services underwent many alterations over the years, were eventually renamed "The Ritual," and remained in the *Discipline* until 1968. Jesse Lee, one of the early Methodist clergy, explained the *Sunday Service's* disappearance in that many of his fellow ministers felt "they could pray better, and with more devotion

---

2. For copies of the original printing of these pages see Appendixes I and II.

while their eyes were shut, than they could with their eyes open. After a few years the prayer book was laid aside, and has never been used since in public worship."[3] Its popularity in England was more durable as evidenced by fifteen additional printings in the first half of the nineteenth century. But the services were retained in the *Discipline*—baptism of infants and adults, eucharist, weddings, funerals, and ordinations—and have been the permanent basis of those rites for American Methodists until today.

In undertaking prayer book revision, Wesley was indulging in a popular eighteenth-century pastime. No previous English prayer book had lasted in legal use for more than half a century, but the 1662 BCP was already into the third decade of its second century. It is still in use in England today. Anglicans, dissenters, even Benjamin Franklin, were publishing proposals for revisions. In April, 1754 Wesley had read with considerable sympathy the Puritan proposals for revision made at the Savoy Conference in 1661 prior to publication of the 1662 BCP. Known as the "Exceptions of the Ministers,[4] these consist of ninety-six items on which Puritans of Presbyterian persuasion had tried, mostly in vain, to shape the 1662 BCP. A still earlier Puritan agenda appears in the "Millenary Petition" of 1603. Both documents are reflected at many points in Wesley's service book.

Although the 1662 BCP basically held the line against both the Laudian "high church" party and the Puritans, efforts were not long in appearing for a more comprehensive prayer book. An abortive effort in 1668 led to a more vigorous but equally unsuccessful attempt in 1689 at what might be called a "liturgy of comprehension."[5] The same year saw the suspension of the non-juring bishops and clergy. Freed from the state church, these men increasingly turned to the review of ancient liturgies, recovering many items overlooked in the English liturgical tradition. Nor were the non-jurors the only connoisseurs of early liturgies. As the scientific study of liturgies began to develop late in the seventeenth century, ancient texts that were

3. *A Short History of the Methodists* (Baltimore: Magill and Clime, 1810), p. 107.
4. Cf. Edward Cardwell, *A History of Conferences* (Oxford: University Press, 1849), pp. 303-35.
5. T. J. Fawcett, *The Liturgy of Comprehension, 1689* (London: Alcuin Club, 1973).

not available to the compilers of 1662 became known. Writers of a variety of theological complexions produced their own proposals, often reflecting more liberal attitudes to doctrinal statements in line with the age of reason.

William Whiston, a mathematician and Anglican clergyman, adapted the fourth-century *Apostolic Constitutions* in 1713 to produce *The Liturgy of the Church of England, Reduc'd Nearer to the Primitive Standards*. Wesley had read (with major reservations) the 1749 plea for reform of a fellow Anglican priest, John Jones, which was contained in his much-discussed *Free and Candid Disquisitions Relating to the Church of England and the Means of Advancing Religion Therein*. A private revision of the BCP with Unitarian leanings was published in 1774 by Theophilus Lindsey, an Anglican priest turned Presbyterian minister. Lindsey combined materials from Samuel Clarke, John Jones, and others with his own ideas to produce *The Book of Common Prayer Reformed According to the Plan of the Late Dr. Samuel Clarke*. Many other attempts at private revision were familiar to Wesley as well as recently prepared services in actual use in the Episcopal Church of Scotland.

The efforts of all these disparate groups—Puritans, comprehensionists, non-jurors, scholars of ancient liturgies, and theological liberals—were known and read by Wesley. Evidences of his familiarity with a variety of sources appear in his revision, indicating that it is a well-researched effort, not personal whim. Wesley apparently refers to the Puritan "Exceptions" of 1661 in a letter of 1755: "Those ministers who truly feared God near an hundred years ago had undoubtedly much the same objections to the Liturgy which some (who never read their Works) have now. And I myself so far allow the force of several of those objections that I should not dare to declare my assent and consent to that book in the terms prescribed."[6] The oath of "unfeigned assent and consent to all and everything contained and prescribed" in the 1662 book had led to the ejection from their churches of both of Wesley's grandfathers. Ordained as fellow of a college, Wesley had not been put to the same test. But the suffering of his Puritan ancestors is vindicated in Wesley's service book.

6. *Letters*, III, 152.

Although the Puritan "Exceptions" underlie many of Wesley's revisions, by no means does he limit himself or always concur in them. The *Sunday Service* reflects far more than just the Puritan strain, although that certainly is present. Had Wesley's book been available a century and a quarter earlier, it might well have been acceptable to many desiring a comprehensive national church.

In a paper prepared for the Conference in 1755,[7] Wesley cited some of his objections to the BCP: the "damnatory clauses" in the Athanasian Creed, laudatory references to Charles II, the answers of the sponsors in baptism, confirmation itself, the absolution in the visitation of the sick, the thanksgiving prayer in the burial of the dead, anything pertaining to differences between bishops and presbyters in the ordinal, and the mention of "whosesoever sins ye remit, they are remitted" in the ordination of priests. All these features vanish in his own revision done almost thirty years later.

It is obvious that Wesley also had a concern for brevity and shortened many items. A major problem was the Anglican practice of actually reading three services each Sunday morning: morning prayer, the litany, and the first portion of the holy communion or ante-communion (known then as the "second service"). As Wesley indicated in his preface, "The service of the LORD'S DAY, the length of which has been often complained of, is considerably shortened." Wesley's proposal still seems lengthy to modern eyes: he shortened morning prayer, relegated the litany to Wednesdays and Fridays only, and abbreviated the ante-communion. But, on the other hand, he advised "the elders to administer the supper of the Lord on every Lord's day." Abridgment occurs, but it is in order to accommodate that rarity in eighteenth-century Anglicanism, a weekly eucharist. Hence it seems more accurate to refer to Wesley's book as a "revision" rather than as an "abridgment." Priorities have been shifted from those manifested by conventional Anglican practice of the time in order to achieve a weekly eucharist.

Despite his own disclaimer in the 1789 letter, Wesley's

---

7. Cf. "Ought We to Separate from the Church of England?" in Frank Baker's *John Wesley and the Church of England* (Nashville: Abingdon Press, 1970), p. 331.

services, like those of most of his contemporary revisers, reflect 120 years of change in the English language itself. Not only is the Lord's Prayer updated, but elsewhere phrases such as "who be" are modernized to "who are" and "charity" frequently becomes "love." There is wholesale redistribution of punctuation marks throughout, especially commas and semicolons, so that readings are recast in more current cadences. Needless to say, all references to the British government or the Church of England disappear or are replaced by American equivalents. The *Sunday Service* is an up-to-date version of the familiar 1662 BCP even though it retains so much of the earlier volume. Wesley's conservatism is moderated by the need to be contemporary.

II

Wesley's service book is a prime source for liturgical theology, i.e., theology based on the liturgical witness to faith. The distinctive elements of the whole Wesleyan movement are shown in the way Wesley orders worship. The *Sunday Service* thus provides important data for theological reflection today. The liturgical circle begins by observing that which is said and done in worship as a reflection of belief, then examines systematically such evidence of faith, and finally reforms worship itself so as to express that faith more adequately. We can only briefly sketch here the evidence to faith found in the *Sunday Service*, and shall not discuss its contribution to liturgical reform at all. (The "Articles of Religion," as revised by Wesley, are an entirely different kind of evidence of belief, one which we shall not consider here.) Wesley's liturgical documentation of faith stands as a challenge in our day, both to theological reflection and to the reform of worship.

The basic pattern, of course, remains that of Anglican practice and faith. Wesley, in his preface, testifies to belief that the prayer book was not exceeded in terms of "solid, scriptural, rational Piety" by any other liturgy whether ancient or modern. Yet his emendations of the BCP are systematic and consistent. The faith that Wesley witnesses to in these pages is obviously uncomfortable with some aspects of prevailing piety and thoroughly at home with others. Rather than analyze Anglican piety in general, we must be content to look more closely at those elements in which Wesley differed from the BCP and made his differences evident by revision. We shall try to deduce his liturgical theology on the basis of what he retains, revises, and omits.

First of all, Wesley's vision for the Christian life is firmly built upon the God-given means of grace, particularly sacrament, scripture, and prayer. (Fasting is mentioned once, for "all Fridays in the Year, except Christmas-day.") Wesley's pattern for the Christian life is based on a community gathering each Sunday for morning and evening prayer, and celebrating the Lord's Supper "on every Lord's day." At a time when most Anglican parishes were content with three eucharists per year, Wesley's advice and his own practice were indeed revolutionary. He himself was not content with only a weekly eucharist but communed, more often than not, twice a week.[8]

Scripture there was in abundance in Wesley's services: a lesson from the Old Testament was provided for each Sunday both for morning and evening prayer in his table of proper lessons; abundant psalmody was arranged over a thirty-day period; and the liturgical epistles and gospels were retained as provided in the BCP. A note suggests that a gospel chapter be read at morning prayer and an epistle chapter at evening prayer. By far the largest portions of the book are devoted to selections from Scripture.

Prayer, too, abounds, not only in the Lord's Day services but in the litany for use on Wednesdays and Fridays and the call for extempore prayer on all other days. The *Sunday Service* calls for a highly disciplined life, structured on the appointed means of grace and lived in Christian community.

The whole focus of the book is strongly christological. Gone is the entire sanctoral (saints' days) cycle. Wesley felt that "most of the holy-days (so called)" were "at present answering no valuable end." Even the abbreviation "St." disappears with few exceptions (pp. 133, 298). The focus, instead, is on Sunday as the day of resurrection, or "Lord's Day," as the Puritans demanded and Wesley often calls it. Even some of the christological festivals such as Epiphany, Maundy Thursday, and All Saints' Day disappear together with the Epiphany, pre-Lenten, and

---

8. John Bowmer, *The Sacrament of the Lord's Supper in Early Methodism* (London: Dacre Press, 1951), p. 55.

Lent seasons. The year focuses on the birth and resurrection cycles, with Sundays numbered after Christmas and Easter as well as after Trinity Sunday. The only exceptions to this exclusively Sunday scheme (all of them christological) are Christmas Day, Good Friday, and Ascension Day.

For the Lord's Day, the traditional Anglican lections and collects are retained with only minor adjustment to accommodate Wesley's method of numbering Sundays after Christmas until "The Sunday next before Easter." It is significant that the Sunday lectionaries for morning and evening prayer and the eucharist are left intact. Christ's work is presented in orderly and systematic recital as the basis for reading and preaching.

Wesley did, however, take to pruning the Psalter rather severely. Of the 150 psalms in BCP, he excises 34 (or more than a fifth) entirely. Verses disappear from another 58, to make a shrinkage from 2,502 verses in the BCP to 1,625 in the *Sunday Service*. This means a move from about 42 verses per service in the BCP to just under 28. William N. Wade[9] has analyzed the deletions as falling into five general categories: curses, wrath, killing, and war; descriptions of the wicked, lack of faith, or special personal circumstances; at odds with salvation by faith; concerns exclusively historical or geographical, especially pertaining to Jerusalem; and references to the use of instruments of dance in worship. Wesley defended his excisions, stating that there were "many Psalms left out, and many parts of the others, as being highly improper for the mouths of a Christian Congregation." He also occasionally made changes in the translation, using the King James Version for a verse when it made better sense.

Wesley certainly is not the first (nor the last) to be troubled by untoward portions of the Psalter.[10] His preference for literal interpretation makes allegory unpalatable, and so he prunes away what seems inappropriate for common worship. The high value Wesley placed on the "Select Psalms" should not be overlooked, for they are by far the largest single item in the *Sunday Service*. Wesley had recited the psalms daily throughout

---

9. Cf. his important dissertation: "A History of Public Worship in the Methodist Episcopal Church and Methodist Episcopal Church, South from 1784 to 1905" (University of Notre Dame, 1981), pp. 52-76.

10. A topic on the agenda of the first synod of Roman Catholic bishops in 1967.

his life. They were a major ingredient in his personal formation, and he intended to transmit such a tradition, reformed to make it even better.

Ever since 1603 the Puritans had urgd that "canonical Scriptures only be read in the Church." Wesley consistently avoids readings from the Apocrypha with one exception: Tobit 4:8-9 is retained as an offertory sentence at the eucharist, although the previous verse is eliminated. No mention of the Apocrypha appears in the "Articles of Religion."

Wesley's perception of the nature of ministry is apparent throughout the book. He prefers the term "Minister" in morning and evening prayer, the litany, and the occasional services. Only in the eucharist and at a few points in the ordinal is "elder" specified. The "superintendant" [sic] has a special ministry as indicated throughout the ordinal, and a "deacon" is designated to read the gospel at his own ordination. There are significant shifts away from signs of priestly power. The words "priest" or "curate" disappear completely as the Puritans had argued in 1661 they should. "Bishop" also has been eliminated completely. No references to clerical garb or ornaments appears.

The term "absolution" has gone entirely. Wesley declared in *Popery Calmly Considered:* "For judicially to pardon sin and absolve the sinner, is a power God has reserved to himself." At morning and evening prayer, the collect from the 24th Sunday after Trinity is substituted for the absolution; at the eucharist the absolution is made into a prayer by changing the pronouns to "thy" and "thou," while the elder identifies with the people by use of "us" instead of "you."

More freedom is allowed the minister in some instances.. The elder "if he see it expedient, may put up an Extempore Prayer" at the eucharist (although unmentioned elsewhere in the services). The Puritans had pled in vain for such freedom. Likewise a sermon is to be preached at the eucharist. Wesley eliminates any mention of using one of the printed homilies from the sixteenth century which BCP suggested. The rather tedious exhortations are scrapped at eucharist and baptism. Sixteenth-century didacticism has been put to rest in these instances, although similar elements, such as the Decalogue at the eucharist or charges at matrimony and at ordination, are retained.

A significant shift occurs in the way the process of becoming a

Christian is signified. The concept of baptismal regeneration, although biblical (John 3:5; Titus 3:5) is problematic for Wesley because of his emphasis on the personal experience of conversion. Wesley keeps the declaration in the "Articles of Religion" that baptism "is a sign of regeneration, or the new birth." But he does make more moderate the references to baptismal regeneration in the rites of infant and adult baptism themselves without eliminating such references altogether. The opening statement in the infant baptism rite and the prayer after the gospel both refer to regeneration as taking place in baptism. But after the act of baptism, in the statement after the signation "that *this Child is* regenerate and grafted," the words "regenerate and" disappear. In the prayer after the Lord's Prayer, "that it hath pleased thee to regenerate *this Infant* with thy Holy Spirit" Wesley removes the words "to regenerate . . . with thy Holy Spirit." Presumption that regeneration is inevitable seems offensive to Wesley, and so any suggestion of such is abolished. Similar disappearances occur in the adult rite: "that *these Persons* are regenerate" loses "regenerate and," and the "now" in "that being now born again" vanishes. In short, Wesley does not eliminate the concept of baptismal regeneration but seems to remove any presumption on it. The 1786 edition makes further changes. Criticism of the doctrine of baptismal regeneration was common in liberal theological circles in Wesley's time and broke out in the Gorham dispute within the Church of England in the 1840s.

Wesley's omissions are often important statements themselves. The most baffling of these is his omission of a rite of confimation. Eighty years later, the Methodist Episcopal Church found it advisable to add a service for the "Reception of Members" and a century after that this was renamed "Confirmation." The value of a separate rite of confirmation has long been problematic. The Puritans had asked in the Millenary Petition of 1603 that "confirmation, as superfluous, may be taken away." Apparently it had been little administered prior to the reign of James I. Wesley indicated his opposition to confirmation in his paper for the Conference in 1755. Perhaps Wesley anticipated the misgivings of modern theologians about confirmation and felt it better to exclude it rather than to perpetuate the mistakes of the middle ages and reformation. At any rate, exclude it he did but with no mention of his reasons for so doing.

Wesley's other omissions are significant but less puzzling. The legal documents often bound in eighteenth-century BCPs, the table of contents, the various Acts of Uniformity, "the Preface," "Concerning the Service of the Church," "Of Ceremonies," and the instructions on reading the Psalter and scripture lessons, Wesley recognized as irrelevant to the American situation. The daily calendar and tables and rules for the feasts and fasts were not necessary for a Sunday service book. Like many of his contemporaries, Wesley was happy to be rid of the so-called Athanasian Creed.

Private baptism he omitted without indicating just why. Probably Wesley had a sound liturgical instinct that baptism ought to be public. The catechism requisite to confirmation also disappears. Similarly absent is visitation of the sick although Wesley keeps communion of the sick. "The Thanksgiving of Women after Childbirth" disappears. Wesley eliminated Ash Wednesday so there is no need for "A Commination, or Denouncing of God's Anger and Judgments against Sinners," appointed for that day. "Forms of Prayer to be used at Sea" also is removed.

It should be no surprise that the vehemently nationalistic state services, included by royal edict in eighteenth-century BCPs, should be removed. Gunpowder treason, the execution of one English monarch, the restoration of another, and the accession of a third (and the hated George III at that) would hardly appeal to Americans. Episcopalians toyed with services for July 4 and Thanksgiving Day, but only the latter made it into their 1789 book. Wesley did not try to anticipate American festivals but otherwise accommodated to a new country and its distinctive situation.

NOTES

Letter of Sept. 10, 1784. This letter appears in most, but not all, surviving copies, sometimes bound before the title page, sometimes after it.

Title page. The name of the publisher, William Strahan, is omitted.

Preface, p. [1]. This preface is found in most copies but not all. At least four different printings survive.

Proper LESSONS to be read at Morning and Evening Prayer, pp. [3-5]. Wesley omits the usual BCP instructions ("the Order how"), the daily calendar, and the tables and rules of the feasts. Only three pages of twenty dealing with propers survive. The thirty-three BCP holy days have largely disappeared, and the three that remain (other than Sundays) are referred to on page [5] simply as "particular Days" instead of "Holy-Days." "Ash-Wednesday" has been removed from Wesley's "Proper PSALMS on certain Days." The Puritan "Exceptions" of 1661 urged "that the religious observation of saints-days appointed to be kept as holy-days, and the vigils thereof, without any foundation (as we conceive) in Scripture, may be omitted." The lessons for the three "particular Days" Wesley retains remain unchanged. Of the "Proper PSALMS on certain Days" six psalms disappear, all ones Wesley removes from his Psalter: 21, 54, 88, 108, 110, and 132.

The most radical change in the table of lessons is in the calendar. The seasons of Epiphany, Pre-Lent, and Lent have been expunged in favor of numbering fifteen Sundays after Christmas plus the "Sunday before Easter" (Lent 6). The missing Sunday is Lent 5. This leaves Wesley short one Sunday, although this would be a problem only in years when Easter came later than mid-April. The idea may have come from Whiston's revision of 1713 which numbered Sundays after Epiphany right through Lent. Other than this one drastic change before Easter, Wesley's calendar is that of the BCP for Sundays. Wesley's suppression of Lent is in line with a long succession of Puritan objections, including the "Exceptions" against "the observation of Lent as a religious fast, the example of Christ's fasting forty days and nights being no more imitable, nor intended for the imitation of a Christian, than any other of his miraculous works were."

Wesley has updated "Mattins" and "Evensong" in the table to "Morning" and "Evening." Wesley's only changes in the lessons themselves are to leave out Exodus 3 and 5 (previously Lent 5). Genesis 7 and 18 are substituted for Genesis 9:1-20 and Genesis 12 on the eleventh Sunday and Genesis 24 and 37 take the place of Genesis 27 and Genesis 34 on the thirteenth Sunday. Genesis 44 is added to Genesis 45 on the fifteenth Sunday. The only clear pattern in Wesley's alterations of lessons seems to be the desire to find more edifying passages in place of some less so, such as Genesis 34.

Wesley added a rubric about the New Testament lesson. This rubric is a great simplification of the daily lectionary in "The Calendar with the Table of Lessons" which Wesley omits. Apparently, for Wesley's Sunday services the lessons to be read "in regular Rotation" indicates readings chosen at the minister's discretion and no indication is given as to the meaning of "where it is otherwise provided." An abridgment of a similar rubric in BCP on fasting is shortened by excluding Lent, the Ember Days, and the three Rogation Days but retaining the Friday fast.

The ORDER for MORNING PRAYER, Every Lord's Day, pp. [7]-14. A major change occurs in the function, as reflected by the subtitle, indicating a weekly service rather than "Daily throughout the Year." Because he proposes an exclusively Sunday service to be used in conjunction with the Lord's Supper, Wesley makes some abridgments. In 1603 the Puritans had urged that "the longsomeness of service [be] abridged," and Wesley noted such a concern in his Preface. Accordingly, the *Venite*, second Lord's Prayer, suffrages, anthem, and two prayers are eliminated and the psalm readings shortened.

But the excisions have been done with a careful hand. The opening rubrics about the place where prayers were to be said and about the ornaments of the church and ministers' garb have disappeared, probably because Wesley found them meaningless in America and unenforced in England. The penitential opening of 1552 survives with a minimum of change: six of the opening sentences vanish for no apparent reason, and a sentence that had listed the acts of worship—confession, thanksgiving, praise, hearing the Word, and petition—disappears from the call to confession. No changes appear in the general confession itself, but the rather didactic BCP absolution has been replaced by the collect for Trinity 24 (unchanged) and the rubrics are made simpler and less priestly. (Theophilus Lindsey's revision of 1774 had substituted the Collect for Purity, instead.)

Deviations are more pronounced in the original 1549 opening

which begins with the Lord's Prayer. The *Venite* and accompanying rubric are omitted altogether even though Psalm 95 appears uncut in Wesley's Psalter. Probably the last four wrathful verses suggested removal of the whole *Venite* to Wesley; these verses were replaced in the 1789 American BCP. The rubric about the *Gloria Patri* omits the words "throughout the year," and apparently it is to be said in unison. The Old Testament lesson is to be found in the weekly "Table of proper Lessons" rather than in the daily Calendar. No rubric about announcing and terminating lessons remains. Likewise gone is the option of the lengthy canticle from the Apocrypha, *Benedicite, omnia opera Domini.* The briefer *Te Deum laudamus* remains. After the second lesson the option of the *Benedictus* (Luke 1:68-79) is lacking, while the *Jubilate Deo* (Psalm 100) survives. The Puritans in 1661 had objected to the *Benedicite* as "apocryphal" and the attempted liturgy of comprehension of 1689 suggested elimination of all New Testament canticles but the *Magnificat*, doubtless in response to Puritan pressures.

The prayers lack the second Lord's Prayer, the suffrages, and the prayers for the royal family and for clergy and people. The second and third collects are no longer daily obligations but remain unchanged to be said weekly, "all devoutly kneeling." No mention is made of an anthem in line with Wesley's conviction that "they cannot properly be called joint worship," nor do the rubrics indicate that any canticles or creed be sung. A shortened version of the prayer for the King's Majesty has become "for the Supreme Rulers." It now intercedes for "the Supreme Rulers of these United States" (the first use of that term in a prayer book). This prayer and that of St. Chrysostom (now untitled) are kept for weekly use. The apostolic benediction, II Corinthians 13:14, remains, except that here and elsewhere Wesley replaces "you" with "us" following more closely the Greek text. The final rubric omits the words "throughout the Year."

The ORDER for EVENING PRAYER, Every Lord's Day., pp. 14-19. Changes parallel to those in morning prayer occur here. After the first lesson, the *Magnificat* (Luke 1:46-55) is not printed but only the second choice, *Cantate Domino*, Psalm 98. Verses 6 and 7 are omitted as in Wesley's Psalter in accord with his omission of reference to musical instruments. After the New Testament lesson, the *Nunc dimittis* (Luke 2:29-32) likewise disappears, leaving *Deus misereatur* (Psalm 67) as the only choice. No reference is made to kneeling for the collects at evening prayer. The Lord's Prayer remains unrevised from BCP here but nowhere else, a slip-up corrected in 1786.

The Athanasian Creed, appointed to be read on thirteen occasions in the year by BCP, disappears entirely. The Puritans had objected to it in 1661 and Wesley in 1755 explained his concurrence in its doctrines but not in "the *damnatory clauses*."

The LITANY, pp. 20-26. The opening rubric omits mention of use on "Sundays, Wednesdays, and Fridays, and at other times," most likely in line with Wesley's concern about the length of the Sunday service. His letter of Sept. 10, 1784 reaffirms the use of the litany on "Wednesdays and Fridays," and it remains in the ordination rites. The petition for King George is redirected to "the Supreme Rulers of these United States." Three subsequent petitions—for the King, royal family, and Lords and nobility— disappear. Another petition, that for "Bishops, Priests, and Deacons," becomes "all the Ministers of thy Gospel." Otherwise the litany remains virtually untouched with the exception of minor emendations.

A PRAYER and THANKSGIVING, to be used every Lord's Day, pp. 26-27. Of the collection of nineteen prayers appointed in BCP, for use at the litany or at morning and evening prayer, Wesley retains for weekly use but two: the "prayer for all conditions of men" and the General Thanksgiving.

THE COLLECTS, EPISTLES, and GOSPELS, To be used throughout the Year, pp. 27-124 (not printed in this edition). Wesley's chief changes are those in the calendar. Gone are all the saints' days plus weekday holy days such as Circumcision, Epiphany, Presentation, Ash Wednesday, Annunciation, All Saints' Day, and the lesser days of Holy Week, Easter Week, and Whitsun Week. Christmas Day, Good Friday, and Ascension Day alone remain. Sundays are numbered "after Christmas" until "The Sunday next before Easter." The BCP collect, epistle, and gospel for the first Sunday after the Epiphany provides Wesley's second Sunday after Christmas propers. (The 1662 BCP had no

Christmas 2 propers, simply reusing Circumcision, which Wesley expunges.) The language of the collects and lections is occasionally updated as in the changes from "charity" to "love" on the Tenth Sunday after Christmas. Anthems are retained to "be said" at morning prayer before the psalms on Easter Day.

The twenty-five Sundays after Trinity remain unchanged except for minor updating of words, punctuation, and capitalization. Except for the removal of holy days and saints days, this is the most conservative part of Wesley's service book and shows his love of the Cranmerian collects and traditional lections. (His treatment of the Psalter is radical by comparison.)

Wesley omits the general rubric about the use of the collect for the vigil or eve of Sundays and holy days. Rubrics about daily use of the Advent 1, Nativity, Circumcision, and Ash Wednesday collects are also missing. A final rubric about the Twenty-fifth Sunday after Trinity is omitted. This BCP rubric provides for the use of propers of unused Sundays after Epiphany if the Trinity Season ran long in any year. The twenty-fifth Sunday's "stir up" collect and lections were to be always "used upon the Sunday next before Advent," another rubric that Wesley omits. At morning and evening prayer he had provided for twenty-six Sundays after Trinity. His scheme for the eucharist could run short some years in the post-Christmas and post-Trinity seasons.

The Order for the Administration of the LORD'S SUPPER, pp. 125-39. See Appendix I for pages 135-36 of what we presume was the first printing. The pages that follow contain the manual acts as probably inserted at Wesley's command. The Puritans generally favored the manual acts, as did most Anglicans, and it is difficult to see why they were retracted in the first printing.

Wesley's treatment of the Lord's Supper is deeply conservative; no really essential matters are altered in it. The long didactic exhortations disappear plus an optional post-communion prayer. Minor adaptations to the American situation occur, but basically the 1662 rite remains intact. Wesley's excision of all the collects printed at the end "to be said after the Offertory, when there is no Communion" is another indication of his determination to have a weekly eucharist.

The title has been shortened, removing the words "or Holy

Communion" but "the Communion" appears in the running heads of each page and "Holy Communion" is in several rubrics. The first three general rubrics are omitted, the first, about giving prior notice of intention to commune, was probably deemed difficult in an itinerant situation and the others, dealing with the "open and notorious evil liver" and unreconciled persons, could be dealt with in Methodist class meetings. The remaining rubric deals with the location of the Lord's table, but Wesley is less specific and eliminates the obsolete reference to north-side celebration, an archaism of the 1662 BCP. Individual rubrics are shortened and simplified throughout and the location of actions is not indicated.

No changes appear in the Decalogue. One of the two collects for the King disappears while the other is altered to "the Supreme Rulers of these United States." The Nicene Creed is omitted, presumably because the Apostles' Creed would have been said already at morning prayer. A long rubric about announcements is omitted and a sermon is mandatory (as the "Exceptions" urged it should be), and no mention is made of the printed homilies. Of the twenty offertory sentences BCP provides, Tobit 4:7 is omitted but the 4:8-9 verses remain, the only use of the Apocrypha in the *Sunday Service* and a passage specifically decried by the "Exceptions." A different translation of I Timothy 6:6-7 is provided. The rubric about the placing of the bread and wine upon the table, a rubric which suggests the possibility of no communion, disappears entirely.

The prayer for the "Whole State of Christ's Church" is altered only to revise allusions to King George, "the whole Council," and to "Bishops and Curates." Wesley apparently felt that the people called Methodists had no need for the long exhortations BCP provides to give "warning" of an upcoming celebration of the holy communion (especially when he desired weekly celebrations), about lax attendance at the sacrament, or for serious preparation for reception of the sacrament. The invitation is unchanged but in the general confession, the sentence: "The burden of them is intolerable" disappears, as it had in Lindsey's 1774 version. The absolution is turned into a prayer by adding "O" and by changing the pronouns (again, following Lindsey on the pronouns). Wesley, who removed many references to posture, adds an "all standing" rubric for the

Comfortable Words and "The People also kneeling" for the Prayer of Humble Access.

The eucharistic prayer remains untouched save for the removal of a redundant "one" in the post-*Sanctus*. All references to weekday celebration are excluded from the proper prefaces as in the "Exceptions." In the preface for Christmas Day: "Of the substance of the Virgin Mary his mother" is removed. The rubric which comes just before the Prayer of Consecration fails to mention "ordering" the bread and wine. Wesley places the fraction three words later than in BCP.

In the communion rubric, "all meekly kneeling," so offensive to the Puritans, disappears. A theological shift occurs in the rubric about reconsecration: Wesley opts for repeating the entire so-called "Prayer of Consecration" rather than just the words of institution (BCP), indicating a move away from the medieval and Lutheran attitude that the verba effected consecration rather than the whole act of thanksgiving. (This had the support of the 1689 attempt at revision, Whiston, and the Scottish communion rite of 1764.)

The original conclusion of the eucharistic prayer in 1549 is retained as a post-communion prayer and the other option, the 1549 post-communion prayer, is dropped (as in Lindsey.) The *Gloria in excelsis* is said, not sung. A new rubric now provides for "Extempore Prayer" if the elder "see it expedient." The concluding blessing adds the word "May" to make it more of a prayer than a benediction. Wesley omits nine rubrics dealing with occasions without communion, the necessary number of communicants, provision, quality, and consumption of the bread and wine, mandatory communion thrice yearly, and money offerings. Gone also is the 1662 statement about kneeling which declares "no adoration is intended" to the bread and wine. Wesley expected the singing of eucharistic hymns, but they are not mentioned in the service itself.

The MINISTRATION of BAPTISM of INFANTS, pp. 139-43. See Appendix II for pages 141-44 of what is presumably the first printing. In the pages that follow, the signation occurs.

Major changes, theological and practical, occur in the rite of infant baptism. The doctrine of baptismal regeneration is not expressed after baptism but is clearly stated before the act of baptism. Godparents are eliminated although at the baptism there is reference to "Friends of the Child." But neither is mention made of the parents, as the Puritans advocated. The rite is shortened, losing the more didactic elements.

Wesley omits rubrics about baptism being in public on Sundays or holy days as well as the word "PUBLICK" in the title (although it appears in the running heads on each page) and the subtitle "To be used in the CHURCH" disappears. He provides no service for "The MINISTRATION of PRIVATE BAPTISM of Children IN HOUSES," probably not wanting to encourage such practice and in accord with the "Exceptions" mention of "no need" for such a rite. No provisions are made for emergency baptism. Gone also are rubrics about godparents and about giving the curate forewarning and being ready after the last lesson at morning or evening prayer. The opening question: "Hath this Child been already baptized, or no?" is eliminated, probably as unnecessary.

Wesley's rite follows unchanged the BCP address which mentions regeneration by water and Spirit. The "flood" prayer is almost untouched as is the succeeding collect with its mention of "spiritual regeneration" despite Puritan exception to these very words. After the gospel (Mark 10:13-16) the exhortation is removed but the following prayer with petition "that *he* may be born again" remains. The address to the godparents disappears together with the renunciation and questions as to faith (the Apostles' Creed) and ethics, responded to formerly by godparents. Almost thirty years before Wesley had objected to "the answers . . . made by the sponsors." The prayers after the creed remain unchanged.

The prayer over the font (lost in American Methodism from 1916 to 1976) remains scarcely changed from BCP. Wesley's conservatism is evident in retaining the rubric about baptism by dipping, a practice going into disuse in Anglicanism at that time. But he does give sprinkling as an alternative and subsequent editions recover the BCP option of pouring. The signation occurs unchanged except for a superfluous "do." As early as the Millenary Petition of 1603, the Puritans had objected to "the cross in baptism" as well as "interrogatories ministered to infants" (which Wesley does omit). The sign of the cross along with kneeling at the eucharist were the object of the most vehement of Puritan objections, and it is remarkable that Wesley (apparently) retains the signation in 1784 but was presuaded to relinquish it in subsequent editions.

The theology of regeneration is moderated in the post-baptismal prayers. In the first, a blunt statement of regeneration—"regenerate and"—disappears as do the words, to which the Puritans had objected, "regenerate . . . with thy Holy Spirit" from the final prayer. Gone also is the final exhortation to the godparents about teaching the catechism and bringing the child to confirmation. Two final rubrics vanish, those concerning children dying baptized and explaining the sign of the cross by referring to the canons of 1604.

The Ministration of BAPTISM to such as are of RIPER YEARS, pp. 143-49. This rite, new to the Church of England in 1662, reflects its growing awareness of mission. In Wesley's version, changes take place similar to those at infant baptism, except that there is no mention whatsoever of signation. The phrase "And able to answer for themselves" disappears from the title. Wesley omits the opening rubrics about notification of the bishop, time of celebration, and previous baptism, all of little necessity in America. No changes appear in the opening address, flood prayer, second prayer, and gospel (John 3:1-8). The exhortation is removed but the following prayer that "*they* may be born again" remains. Minor changes happen in the address to the candidates. Wesley retains the renunciation and credal and ethical questions with "flesh" changed to "body" in the Creed. The prayers which follow remain intact.

Only the reference to godparents is changed in the baptismal rubrics. Dipping or pouring is specified, with no mention of sprinkling. All reference to the sign of the cross is missing. In the three final prayers, "regenerate and" disappears from the first and the "now" is removed in the third from the phrase "being now born again." Two final exhortations to godparents and the new Christians are removed, as well as two final rubrics on confirmation and the baptism of children older than infants.

Two significant omissions occur in subsequent pages: Wesley's removal of "A CATECHISM" and that for which it prepared, "THE ORDER OF CONFIRMATION." Wesley's actions are clear in removing confirmation, but his reasons are not.

The Form of Solemnization of MATRIMONY, pp. 149-55. Wesley changes little in the marriage service although he does omit the giving away of the bride, the exchange of rings, the psalms, and the final exhortation. A surprising survival is the reading of the banns, although no mention is made of reading them at the offertory at the second service (BCP). Legal details about the banns disappear from the rubrics, as well as all indications that the first part of the service takes place "In the body of the Church." The address to the congregation survives intact contrary to Wesley's usual removal of didactic exhortations. The long rubric about impediments is excised.

The betrothal vows are unchanged and lead immediately into the nuptial vows with no giving-away ceremony, a change for which Wesley seems to have no precedent. In the second vows "troth" becomes "Faith" and a "be" is added: "take thee M. to be my . . . ." The long rubric and words which accompany the giving of the ring are absent, as is any reference to this action in the prayer and pronouncement that follow. The Millenary Petition of 1603 had asked that "the ring in marriage . . . may be corrected" and the "Exceptions" reiterate this.

The service is shortened after the blessing by elimination of Psalm 128 or 67, although Wesley printed both in his Psalter. No rubric mentions the move to the Lord's table which the 1662 BCP had retained despite Puritan protests. Only minor changes appear in the *Kyrie*, Lord's Prayer, suffrages, and the three final prayers. Wesley makes no mention of a sermon and removes the long exhortation on "the duties of Man and Wife." The final rubric, advising the couple to receive communion then or shortly thereafter, is removed as the Puritans had suggested it be.

Wesley omits altogether "THE ORDER FOR The VISITATION of the SICK." He had objected in 1755 to "the *absolution* in the Office for visiting the sick," an objection his Puritan forebears had raised in 1661.

The COMMUNION of the SICK, pp. 155-56. Wesley's rite is identical with the brief Anglican rite, lacking only the long introductory rubric which gives details about circumstances of celebration and where to begin, and the three last of the final rubrics on the impossibility of communing in certain situations, the use of the visitation rite, and "in time of Plague, Sweat," or such contagion.

The Order for the BURIAL of the DEAD, pp. 156-61. Beyond omission of the committal and thanksgiving, only minor changes take place in this rite. Most references to location in church or churchyard are missing. The opening rubric, disallowing the use of the service for the unbaptized, excommunicate, or suicides, is deleted. The choice of psalms is reduced to one (Psalm 90) although BCP gives Psalm 39 first and Wesley does include it in his Psalter. The psalm and epistle (I Corinthians 15:20-58) have minor changes in translation.

The rubric after the epistle presumes that the previous part of the service was held inside the church but abbreviates the BCP wording. The committal is omitted together with the rubric about casting earth. The prayer which follows the Lord's Prayer is removed, Wesley having complained in 1755 about "the thanksgiving in the *Burial Office*." Absent from the final collect are two clauses: "who also hath taught us, by his holy Apostle Saint Paul, not to be sorry, as men without hope, for them that sleep in him" and "as our hope is this our *brother* doth." Wesley may have hesitated to sound so certain about the eternal destination of the departed as these deleted items suggest. The Puritan "Exceptions" had feared that these items might "harden the wicked" and urged their revision.

Two other pastoral offices are omitted: "THE Thanksgiving of Women after Child-birth" and "A COMMINATION OR Denouncing of God's Anger and Judgments against Sinners." The first is a short office consisting of Psalm 116 or 127 (to which Wesley took no exception), *Kyrie*, Lord's Prayer, suffrages, and prayer of thanksgiving. Wesley's reasons for omitting this service are unclear. Since he had eliminated Ash Wednesday and Lent, no purpose would be served by the commination rite. Wesley must have found repugnant its curses from Deuteronomy 27, for he had removed similar images of divine wrath from the Psalter. (Lindsey also deleted both services).

SELECT PSALMS, pp. 162-279 (not printed in this edition). The largest single item in Wesley's service book is his abridgment and editing of "The PSALTER OR PSALMS of DAVID, Pointed as they are to be sung, or said in Churches." Wesley retains the daily distribution of psalms for both morning and evening prayer over a thirty-day period. He omits the Latin titles for each psalm.

Wesley eliminates entirely thirty-four psalms (14, 21, 52, 53, 54, 58, 60, 64, 72, 74, 78, 79, 80, 81, 82, 83, 87, 88, 94, 101, 105, 106, 108, 109, 110, 120, 122, 129, 132, 134, 136, 137, 140, and 149). In addition, portions of 58 others disappear. (The chief reasons for these deletions have been listed in the Introduction.) The net result is to reduce the number of verses read by about one third. Wesley numbers the verses retained consecutively with no indications of verses omitted. Occasionally the BCP translation is replaced by that of the King James Version.

For reasons unknown, Wesley omitted completely "Forms of PRAYER to be used at SEA." The prayers for "His Majesty's Navy" obviously would have had little appeal to Americans.

The Form and Manner of making of DEACONS, pp. 280-85. In many printings of the BCP, the ordinal is omitted. Where present, an entire page is often given to the title and "THE PREFACE." The BCP preface defends a three-fold ministry, gives minimum ages for each ministry, and speaks to the examination of candidates and times of ordination. Wesley makes a distinction from the rest of the service book simply by two large rules at the top of the page, similar to those which mark off the "Articles of Religion" on page 306. His title for the whole ordinal dispenses with the words "and Consecrating" and "According to the Order of the Church of England." Here and elsewhere, Wesley changes "Bishops" to "Superintendants" [*sic*] and "Priests" to "Elders." Throughout he removes all reference to the English Church and its structures and changes "Ordering" to "Ordaining." All references to clerical garb are struck from the rubrics. All three services begin with morning prayer, and the ordinations are all in the context of holy communion. For the ordination of deacons and elders, the sermon follows morning prayer; for superintendents, it comes after the gospel.

The rite of deacons begins (after abbreviated rubrics) without the presentation. Wesley omits reprinting the litany (pp. 20-26). BCP reprints it, adding a new petition for deacons (or priests) but omitting the final prayer and benediction. Wesley retains these last two items but excludes them (by rubric) in the elders' rite. The order of the whole service is similar to that of the usual Sunday practice of the Church of England—morning prayer, litany, and eucharist—and leads naturally to the collect for the eucharist.

The collect and epistle (I Timothy 3:8-13) are unchanged although the alternative (Acts 6:2-7) is missing. The "Oath of the Kings Sovereignty" necessarily disappears. Changes in the examination reflect the American situation with the total effect that the deacon's duties and whereabouts are less circumscribed. The duty of expounding the scriptures is added without qualification and "read homilies" deleted.

The laying on of hands does not specify that the candidates kneel and, in the formula, "committed unto thee" is omitted. The words at the deliverance of the Bible (not the "New Testament" as in BCP) do not limit preaching by the phrase "if thou be thereto licensed by the bishop himself." The gospel is the same (Luke 12:35-38) and Wesley indicates that communion is to follow immediately, not just "the same day." Wesley removes the final rubric about waiting a year before being ordained priest.

The Form and Manner of ordaining of ELDERS, pp. 285-96. Many of the same changes are made for elders as for deacons although the rubrics are less altered. The chief theological change is in the omission from the formula at the laying on of hands: "Whose sins thou dost forgive, they are forgiven; and whose sins thou dost retain, they are retained" (John 20:23). Wesley had objected to this in 1755 on theological grounds. The restriction to ministering in the congregation "where thou shall be lawfully appointed thereunto" could hardly survive the scrutiny of one who deemed the whole world his parish. The shorter alternative gospel, Matthew 9:36-38, and the Nicene Creed are also omitted.

The second rubric is shortened as is the presentation. A new rubric is added: "their Names being read aloud." The inquiry about impediments speaks of "this day to ordain Elders," instead of "to receive this day into the holy Office of Priesthood." A clause is dropped from the epistle (Ephesians 4:7-13). Curiously the long exhortation remains, only one word being changed. The third question of the examination is shortened drastically and, in the fourth, "Cures" becomes

34

"district." Only one translation, that of Bishop Cosin, is given here and at the superintendents' rite for the *Veni, Creator Spiritus*. The communion rubric and final rubric are simplified.

The Form of Ordaining of a SUPERINTENDANT, pp. 296-305. Much in the title changes but little in the service itself. Wesley's title is an abridgment of "The FORM of Ordaining or Consecrating OF AN ARCHBISHOP OR BISHOP: Which is always to be performed upon some SUNDAY or HOLY-DAY." Throughout, Wesley drops the term "consecrate" and "Superintendant" [*sic*] takes the place of "Archbishop." Elders assist the presiding superintendent in the laying on of hands and perform some of the other functions BCP ascribes to bishops.

The short Timothy 3:1-7 epistle option is dropped. John 20:19-23 disappears as a gospel option, doubtless because of its mention of forgiveness and retention of sins. Wesley, for once, allows two BCP options instead of one: John 21:15-17 or Matthew 28:18-20. The Nicene Creed is absent.

At the presentation the candidate is described as "godly" but Wesley leaves out "and well-learned." The King's Mandate, the Oath of the King's Supremacy, and the Oath of due obedience to the Archbishop have no place in Wesley's version. No petition is added to the litany similar to that which BCP provides for this occasion. At the beginning of the examination "and the ancient Canons" is omitted and "diocese" becomes "district" in the sixth question. In the charge at the giving of the Bible, "and be diligent in doing them" is removed. Wesley makes it clear that "other Persons present" are also to communicate.

Four nationalistic services which in BCP follow are discarded: gunpowder treason, death of Charles I, restoration of Charles II, and accession of George III.

ARTICLES OF RELIGION, pp. 306-41. Wesley's revision of the Articles is one of the most sweeping in the whole book. Thirty-nine articles are reduced to twenty-four (another is added in subsequent editions) and many of the survivors are abridged or altered. As might be expected, the Royal Declaration of George III is omitted. The ratification by convocation in 1571 and the table of the articles also disappear. Wesley's intent in revision seems to be to insist only on central Christian doctrines and to avoid unnecessary controversy.

Those articles which are excised entirely are: Of the going down of Christ into Hell; Of the Three Creeds; Of Works before Justification; Of Christ alone without Sin; Of Predestination and Election; Of obtaining eternal Salvation only by the Name of Christ; Of the Authority of the Church; Of the Authority of General Councils; Of Ministering in the Congregation; Of the Unworthiness of the Ministers, which hinder not the effect of the Sacraments; Of the Wicked, which eat not the Body of Christ in the use of the Lord's Supper; Of excommunicate Persons, how they are to be avoided; Of the Homilies; Of Consecration of Bishops and Ministers; and Of the Civil Magistrates.

We shall follow Wesley's numbering of the remaining articles in examining major changes. In V, all mention of the Apocryphal books disappears. Number VII is much abridged, losing all mention of God's wrath and damnation but vehemently affirming human inclination to evil by adding "and that continually." IX avoids any mention of the homilies. A change is made in the name and contents of XII from "Of Sin after Baptism" to "Of sin after Justification" with the term "justification" substituted throughout for "baptism." A condemnation of the Church of Rome in XIII is dropped. In XVI Wesley omits "sure witnesses and effectual" after "but rather they be certain" and before "Signs of Grace."

Major surgery occurs in XVII. "Christened" becomes "baptized." After "new birth" Wesley omits mention of any benefits received from baptism other than regeneration. The list in BCP includes: "whereby as by an instrument, they that receive Baptism rightly are grafted into the Church; the promises of forgiveness of sin, and of our adoption to be the sons of God by the Holy Ghost, are visibly signed and sealed; Faith is confirmed, and Grace increased by virtue of prayer unto God." In the final sentence, Wesley drops "in any wise" and "as most agreeable with the institution of Christ." The total effect is to weaken somewhat the teaching of the efficacy of baptism. By contrast, Article XVIII, on the Lord's Supper, remains intact.

In XIII "rites and ceremonies" is substituted for "Traditions" and the mention of the magistrate and "man's authority" vanishes. Reference to "certain *Anabaptists*" disappears in XXIII.

"A TABLE of KINDRED and AFFINITY," usually bound in BCPs, is omitted in Wesley' *Sunday Service*. Whereas the usual BCP close is "The End," Wesley, for once, prefers a Latin word as his final word: "FINIS."

SELECT BIBLIOGRAPHY

Baker, Frank. *From Wesley to Asbury*. Durham: Duke University Press, 1976.

———. *John Wesley and the Church of England*. Nashville: Abingdon Press, 1970.

———. *A Union Catalogue of the Publications of John and Charles Wesley*. Durham: Divinity School, Duke University, 1966.

English, John C. "The Sacrament of Baptism according to the Sunday Service of 1784," *Methodist History*, V (January, 1967), 10-16.

Cardwell, Edward. *A History of Conferences and Other Proceedings Connected with the Revision of the Book of Common Prayer from the Year 1558 to the Year 1690*. Third Edition. Oxford: University Press, 1849.

Cuming, G. J. *A History of Anglican Liturgy*. Second Edition. London: Macmillan, 1982.

Fawcett, Timothy J. *The Liturgy of Comprehension of 1689*. London: Alcuin Club, 1973.

Gee, Henry and Hardy, William John. *Documents Illustrative of English Church History*. London: Macmillan & Co., 1910.

George, A. Raymond. "The 'Sunday Service,' " *Proceedings of the Wesley Historical Society*, XL (February, 1976), 137-44.

———. "The Sunday Service of the Methodists," *Communio Sanctorum: Mélangés offerts à Jean Jacques von Allmen*. Geneva: Labor et Fides, 1982, pp. 194-203.

———. "The Sunday Service 1784," *Friends of Wesley Chapel Annual Lecture No. 2*, n.p., 1983.

Grisbrooke, W. Jardine. *Anglican Liturgies of the Seventeenth and Eighteenth Centuries*. London: SPCK, 1958.

Hall, Peter. *Documents Illustrative of the Liturgy of the Church of England*. Vol. VII *Dunkirk Prayer-book*. Bath: Binns and Goodwin, 1848.

———. *Reliquae Liturgicae. Documents Connected with the Liturgy of the Church of England*. Vol. IV *The Savoy Liturgy*. Bath: Binns and Goodwin, 1847.

Harmon, Nolan B. "John Wesley's 'Sunday Service' and its American Revisions," *Proceedings of the Wesley Historical Society*, XXXIX (June, 1974), 137-44.

———. *Rites and Ritual of Episcopal Methodism*. Nashville: Publishing House of the M.E. Church, South, 1926.

Hatchett, Marion J. *The Making of the First American Prayerbook*. Ann Arbor: University Microfilms, 1973; New York: Seabury Press, 1982.

Hunter, Frederick. "Sources of Wesley's Revision of the Prayer Book in 1784-8," *Proceedings of the Wesley Historical Society*, XXIII (1941-42), 123-33.

Peaston, A. Elliott. *The Prayer Book Tradition in the Free Churches*. London: James Clarke & Co., 1964.

Spellman, Norman. "The Formation of the Methodist Episcopal Church," *The History of American Methodism*. Nashville: Abingdon Press, 1964, I, 185-232.

Swift, Wesley F. "John Wesley's Lectionary," *London Quarterly & Holborn Review* CLXXXIII (October, 1958), 298-304.

———. "Methodism and the Book of Common Prayer," *Proceedings of the Wesley Historical Society*, XXVII (1949-50), 33-41.

———. " 'The Sunday Service of the Methodists,' " *Proceedings of the Wesley Historical Society*, XXIX (March, 1953), 12-20.

———. " 'The Sunday Service of the Methodists,' " *Proceedings of the Wesley Historical Society*, XXXII (March, 1960), 97-101.

Thompson, Bard. *Liturgies of the Western Church*. Cleveland: Collins, 1961.

Wesley, John. *The Letters*. Edited by John Telford. London: Epworth Press, 1931. 8 volumes.

To Dr. COKE, Mr. ASBURY, and our Brethren in *NORTH-AMERICA.*

1. **B**Y a very uncommon train of providences, many of the provinces of *North-America* are totally disjoined from their mother-country, and erected into Independent States. The Englifh government has no authority over them either civil or ecclefiaftical, any more than over the States of *Holland.* A civil authority is exercifed over them, partly by the Congrefs, partly by the provincial Affemblies. But no one either exercifes or claims any ecclefiaftical authority at all. In this peculiar fituation fome thoufands of the inhabitants of thefe States defire my advice; and in compliance with their defire, I have drawn up a little fketch.

2. Lord KING's account of the primitive church convinced me many years ago, that Bifhops and Prefbyters are the fame order, and confequently have the fame right to ordain. For many years I have been importuned from time to time, to exercife this right, by ordaining part of our travelling preachers. But I have ftill refufed, not only for peace' fake : but becaufe I was determined, as little as poffible to violate the eftablifhed order of the national church to which I belonged.

a   3. But

3. But the cafe is widely different between England and North-America. Here there are Bifhops who have a legal jurifdiction. In America there are none, neither any parifh minifters. So that for fome hundred miles together there is none either to baptize or to adminifter the Lord's fupper. Here therefore my fcruples are at an end : and I conceive myfelf at full liberty, as I violate no order and invade no man's right, by appointing and fending labourers into the harveft.

4. I have accordingly appointed Dr. Coke and Mr. Francis Asbury, to be joint *Superintendents* over our brethren in North-America : As alfo Richard Whatcoat and Thomas Vasey, to act as *Elders* among them, by baptizing and adminiftering the Lord's fupper. And I have prepared a liturgy little differing from that of the church of England (I think, the beft conftituted national church in the world) which I advife all the travelling-preachers to ufe, on the Lord's day, in all their congregations, reading the litany only on Wednefdays and Fridays, and praying extempore on all other days. I alfo advife the elders to adminifter the fupper of the Lord on every Lord's day.

5. If any one will point out a more ration - al and fcriptural way, of feeding and guiding thofe poor fheep in the wildernefs, I will gladly

gladly embrace it. At prefent I cannot fee any better method than that I have taken.

6. It has indeed been propofed, to defire the Englifh Bifhops, to ordain part of our preachers for *America*. But to this I object, 1. I defired the Bifhop of *London*, to ordain only one; but could not prevail: 2. If they confented, we know the flownefs of their proceedings; but the matter admits of no delay. 3. If they would ordain them *now*, they would likewife expect to govern them. And how grievoufly would this intangle us? 4. As our *American* brethren are now totally difentangled both from the State, and from the Englifh Hierarchy, we dare not intangle them again, either with the one or the other. They are now at full liberty, fimply to fol-low the fcriptures and the primitive church. And we judge it beft that they fhould ftand faft in that liberty, wherewith GOD has fo ftrangely made them free.

JOHN WESLEY.

THE

SUNDAY SERVICE

OF THE

METHODISTS

IN

NORTH AMERICA.

With other Occasional Services.

LONDON:

Printed in the Year MDCCLXXXIV.

I BELIEVE there is no LITURGY in the World, either in ancient or modern language, which breathes more of a folid, fcriptural, rational Piety, than the COMMON PRAYER of the CHURCH of ENGLAND. And though the main of it was compiled confiderably more than two hundred years ago, yet is the language of it, not only pure, but ftrong and elegant in the higheft degree.

Little alteration is made in the following edition of it, (which I recommend to our SOCIETIES in AMERICA) except in the following inftances :

1. Moft of the holy-days (fo called) are omitted, as at prefent anfwering no valuable end.

2. The fervice of the LORD's DAY, the length of which has been often complained of, is confiderably fhortened.

3. Some fentences in the offices of Baptifm, and for the Burial of the Dead, are omitted.—And,

4. Many Pfalms left out, and many parts of the others, as being highly improper for the mouths of a Chriftian Congregation.

John Wefley.

Briftol, Septemben 9,
  1784.

Proper *LESSONS* to be read at *Morning* and *Evening* Prayer, on the *SUNDAYS* throughout the *Year.*				
Sundays of Advent.	*Morning.*		*Evening.*	
The firſt.	Iſaiah —	1	Iſaiah —	2
2 ——	——	5	——	24
3 ——	——	25	——	26
4 ——	——	30	——	32
Sundays after Chriſtmas.				
The firſt	——	37	——	38
2 ——	——	41	——	43
3 ——	——	44	——	46
4 ——	——	51	——	53
5 ——	——	55	——	56
6 ——	——	57	——	58
7 ——	——	59	——	64
8 ——	——	65	——	66
9 ——	Geneſis	1	Geneſis	2
10 ——	——	3	——	6
11 ——	——	7	——	18
12 ——	19 to ver.	30	——	22
13 ——	——	24	——	37
14 ——	——	39	——	42
15 ——	——	43	—— 44 &	45
Sunday before Eaſter.				
1 Leſſon.	Exodus	9	Exodus	10
2 Leſſon.	Matth.	26	Heb. 5 to v.	11
Eaſter day.				
1 Leſſon.	Exodus	12	Exodus	14
2 Leſſon.	Rom.	6	Acts 2 v.	22
Sundays after Eaſter.				
The firſt.	Numb.	16	Numb.	22
2 ——	— 23 &	24	——	25
3 ——	Deuter.	4	——	5
4 ——	——	6	——	7
5 ——	——	8	——	9
Sunday after Aſcenſion day.	——	12	Deuter.	13
Whitſunday.				
1 Leſſon.	—16 to ver.	18	Iſaiah	11
2 Leſſon.	Acts 10 ver.	34	Acts 19 to ver.	21

A 2

Proper Lessons for Sundays.

Trinity-Sunday	Morning.		Evening.	
1 Lesson.	Genesis	1	Genesis	18
2 Lesson.	Matth.	3	1 John	5
Sundays after Trinity Sunday.				
The first.	Joshua	10	Joshua	23
2——	Judges	4	Judges	5
3——	1 Sam.	2	1 Sam.	3
4——	——	12	——	13
5——	——	15	——	17
6——	2 Sam.	12	2 Sam.	19
7——	——	21	——	24
8——	1 Kings	13	1 Kings	17
9——	——	18	——	19
10——	——	21	——	22
11——	2 Kings	5	2 Kings	9
12——	——	10	——	18
13——	——	19	——	23
14——	Jerem.	5	Jerem.	22
15——	——	35	——	36
16——	Ezekiel	2	Ezekiel	13
17——	——	14	——	18
18——	——	20	——	24
19——	Daniel	3	Daniel	6
20——	Joel	2	Micah	6
21——	Habak.	2	Prov.	1
22——	Prov.	2	——	3
23——	——	11	——	12
24——	——	13	——	14
25——	——	15	——	16
26——	——	17	——	19

☞ Let the Second Lesson in the Morning be a Chapter out of the Four Gospels, and the Acts of the Apostles; and the Second Lesson in the Evening be a Chapter out of the Epistles, in regular Rotation; excepting where it is otherwise provided.

Proper LESSONS for particular Days.

	Morning.	Evening.
Nativity of Chrift.		
1 Leffon.	Ifaiah 9 to v. 8	Ifaiah 7 v. 10. to (v. 17
2 Leffon.	Luke 2 to v. 15	Tit. 3 v. 4 to v. 9
Good Friday.		
1 Leffon.	Gen. 22 to v. 20	Ifaiah 53
2 Leffon.	John 18	1 Peter 2
Afcenfion-day.		
1 Leffon.	Deuter. 10	2 Kings 2
2 Leffon.	Luke 24 v. 44.	Eph. 4 to v. 17.

Proper PSALMS on certain Days.

	Morning.	Evening.
Chriftmas-day.	Pfalm 19 ——— 45 ——— 85	Pfalm 89 ——— ———
Good Friday.	Pfalm 22 ——— 40	Pfalm 69 ———
Eafter-day.	Pfalm 2 ——— 57 ——— 111	Pfalm 113 ——— 114 ——— 118
Afcenfion-day.	Pfalm 8 ——— 15	Pfalm 24 ——— 47
Whit-funday.	Pfalm 48 ——— 68	Pfalm 104 ——— 145

Days of Fafting or Abftinence.

All the Fridays in the Year, except Chriftmas-day.

A 3

The ORDER for

MORNING PRAYER,

Every Lord's Day.

At the Beginning of Morning Prayer, the Minifter fhall read with a loud Voice fome one or more of thefe Sentences of the Scriptures that follow : And then he fhall fay that which is written after the faid Sentences.

WHEN the wicked man turneth away from his wickednefs that he hath committed, and doeth that which is lawful and right, he fhall fave his foul alive. *Ezek.* xviii. 27.

The facrifices of God are a broken fpirit : a broken and a contrite heart, O God, thou wilt not defpife. *Pfal.* li. 17.

To the Lord our God belong mercies and forgiveneffes, though we have rebelled againft him : neither have we obeyed the voice of the Lord our God, to walk in his laws which he fet before us. *Dan.* ix. 9, 10.

I will arife, and go to my father, and will fay unto him, Father, I have finned againft Heaven and before thee, and am no more worthy to be called thy fon. *Luke,* xv. 18, 19.

Enter not into judgment with thy fervant, O Lord ; for in thy fight fhall no man living be juftified. *Pfal.* cxliii. 2.

DEarly beloved brethren, the Scripture moveth us, in fundry places, to acknowledge and confefs our manifold fins and wickednefs, and that we fhould not diffemble-or cloke them before the face of Almighty God, our heavenly Father ; but

confefs

confeſs them with an humble, lowly, penitent, and obedient heart; to the end that we may obtain forgiveneſs of the ſame, by his infinite goodneſs and mercy.   Wherefore I pray and beſeech you, as many as are here preſent, to accompany me with a pure heart and humble voice, unto the throne of the heavenly grace, ſaying after me.

A general Confeſſion, to be ſaid by the whole Congregation, after the Miniſter, all kneeling.

ALmighty and moſt merciful Father, We have erred and ſtrayed from thy ways like loſt ſheep. We have followed too much the devices and deſires of our own hearts. We have offended againſt thy holy laws. We have left undone thoſe things which we ought to have done; And we have done thoſe things which we ought not to have done; And there is no health in us. But thou, O Lord, have mercy upon us, miſerable offenders. Spare thou them, O God, which confeſs their faults. Reſtore thou them that are penitent; According to thy promiſes declared unto mankind in Chriſt Jeſus our Lord. And grant, O moſt merciful Father, for his ſake, That we may hereafter live a godly, righteous, and ſober life; To the glory of thy holy Name. Amen.

Then the Miniſter ſhall ſay,

O Lord, we beſeech thee, abſolve thy people from their offences; that, through thy bountiful goodneſs, we may be delivered from the bands of thoſe ſins, which by our frailty we have committed. Grant this, O heavenly Father, for Jeſus Chriſt's ſake, our bleſſed Lord and Saviour.

The People ſhall anſwer here, and at the End of all other Prayers. Amen.

Then

Then the Minister shall say the Lord's Prayer; the People also repeating it with him, both here, and wheresoever else it is used in Divine Service.

OUR Father who art in Heaven, Hallowed be thy Name; Thy kingdom come; Thy Will be done on Earth, As it is in Heaven: Give us this day our daily bread; And forgive us our trespasses, As we forgive them that trespass against us; And lead us not into temptation; But deliver us from evil: For thine is the Kingdom, and the Power, and the Glory, For ever and ever. Amen.

Then likewise he shall say,

O Lord, open thou our lips.
Answ. And our mouth shall shew forth thy praise.
Minist. O God, make speed to save us;
Answ. O Lord, make haste to help us.

Here all standing up, the Minister shall say,

Glory be to the Father, and to the Son, and to the Holy Ghost;
Answ. As it was in the beginning, is now, and ever shall be, world without end. Amen.
Minist. Praise ye the Lord.
Answ. The Lord's Name be praised.

Then shall follow the Psalms, in order as they are appointed. And at the End of every Psalm, shall be repeated,

Glory be to the Father, and to the Son, and to the Holy Ghost;
As it was in the beginning, is now, and ever shall be, world without end. Amen.

Then shall be read distinctly, the First Lesson taken out of the Old Testament, as is appointed in the Table

A 5

of

of proper Leſſons : He that readeth, ſo ſtanding,
and turning himſelf as he may be beſt heard of all.
And after that, ſhall be ſaid the following Hymn :

WE praiſe thee, O God : we acknowledge
thee to be the Lord.

All the earth doth worſhip thee, the Father
everlaſting.

To thee all Angels cry aloud : the Heavens,
and all the powers therein.

To thee Cherubin and Seraphin continually
do cry,

Holy, holy, holy, Lord God of Sabaoth ;

Heaven and Earth are full of the Majeſty of thy
Glory.

The glorious company of the Apoſtles praiſe
thee.

The goodly fellowſhip of the Prophets praiſe
thee.

The noble army of Martyrs praiſe thee.

The Holy Church throughout all the world
doth acknowledge thee ;

The Father of an infinite Majeſty ;

Thine honourable, true, and only Son ;

Alſo the Holy Ghoſt, the Comforter.

Thou art the King of glory, O Chriſt ;

Thou art the everlaſting Son of the Father.

When thou tookeſt upon thee to deliver man,
thou didſt not abhor the Virgin's womb.

When thou hadſt overcome the ſharpneſs of
death, thou didſt open the kingdom of Heaven to
all believers.

Thou ſitteſt at the right hand of God, in the
glory of the Father.

We believe that thou ſhalt come to be our
Judge.

We

We therefore pray thee, help thy servants, whom thou haft redeemed with thy precious blood.

Make them to be numbered with thy Saints in glory everlasting.

O Lord, fave thy people, and blefs thine heritage.

Govern them, and lift them up for ever.

Day by day we magnify thee ;

And we worfhip thy name ever, world without end.

Vouchfafe, O Lord, to keep us this day without fin.

O Lord, have mercy upon us : have mercy upon us.

O Lord, let thy mercy lighten upon us, as our truft is in thee.

O Lord, in thee have I trufted : let me never be confounded.

Then fhall be read in like manner the Second Leffon, taken out of the New Teftament : and after that, the following Pfalm :

O Be joyful in the Lord, all ye lands : ferve the Lord with gladnefs, and come before his prefence with a fong.

Be ye fure that the Lord he is God ; it is he that hath made us, and not we ourfelves : we are his people, and the fheep of his pafture.

O go your way into his gates with thankfgiving, and into his courts with praife : be thankful unto him, and fpeak good of his Name.

For the Lord is gracious, his mercy is everlafting : and his truth endureth from generation to generation.

Glory be to the Father, and to the Son, and to the Holy Ghoft ;

As it was in the beginning, is now, and ever fhall be, world without end. Amen.

A 6

Then

*Then shall be said the Apostles' Creed by the Minister
and the People, standing.*

I Believe in God the Father Almighty, Maker of
Heaven and Earth :
And in Jesus Christ his only Son our Lord ;
Who was conceived by the Holy Ghost ; Born of
the Virgin Mary ; Suffered under Pontius Pilate ;
Was crucified, dead, and buried, He descended
into hell : The third day he rose again from the
dead : He ascended into Heaven, And sitteth on the
right hand of God, the Father Almighty ; From
thence he shall come to judge the quick and the
dead.
I believe in the Holy Ghost ; The Holy Ca-
tholick Church ; The Communion of Saints ;
The Forgiveness of Sins ; The Resurrection of
the Body, And the Life everlasting.   Amen.

*And after that, the Minister shall pronounce with a loud
Voice,*

The Lord be with you ;
Answ. And with thy spirit.

Minister.   Let us pray.
Lord, have mercy upon us.
Answ. Christ have mercy upon us.
Minist. Lord, have mercy upon us.

*Then shall follow three Collects ; the first of the Day,
which shall be the same that is appointed at the
Communion ; the second for Peace ; the third for
Grace to live well ; all devoutly kneeling.*

The second Collect, for Peace.

O God, who art the author of peace, and lover
of concord, in knowledge of whom standeth
our eternal life, whose service is perfect freedom ;
Defend us thy humble servants in all assaults of
6   our

our enemies; that we, furely trufting in thy defence, may not fear the power of any adverfaries, through the might of Jefus Chrift our Lord. *Amen.*

The Third Collect, for Grace.

O Lord our heavenly Father, Almighty and ever-lafting God, who haft fafely brought us to the beginning of this day; Defend us in the fame with thy mighty power; and grant that this day we fall into no fin; neither run into any kind of danger: but that all our doings may be ordered by thy governance, to do always that is righteous in thy fight, through Jefus Chrift our Lord. *Amen.*

Then thefe Prayers following are to be read.

A Prayer for the Supreme Rulers.

O Lord our heavenly Father, high and mighty, King of kings, Lord of lords, the only Ruler of princes, who doft from thy throne behold all the dwellers upon earth; Moft heartily we befeech thee, with thy favour to behold the Supreme Rulers of thefe United States, and fo replenifh them with the grace of thy Holy Spirit, that they may alway incline to thy will, and walk in thy way; through Jefus Chrift our Lord. *Amen.*

ALmighty God, who haft given us grace at this time with one accord, to make our common fupplications unto thee, and doft promife that when two or three are gathered together in thy Name, thou wilt grant their requefts; Fulfil now, O Lord, the defires and petitions of thy fervants, as may be moft expedient for them: granting us in this world knowledge of thy truth, and in the world to come life everlafting. *Amen.*

2 *Cor.*

2 Cor. xiii 14.

THE grace of our Lord Jesus Christ, and the love of God, and the fellowship of the Holy Ghost, be with you all evermore. *Amen.*

Here endeth the Order of Morning Prayer.

The ORDER for
EVENING PRAYER,
Every Lord's Day.

At the Beginning of Evening Prayer, the Minister shall read with a loud Voice some one or more of these Sentences of the Scriptures that follow: And then he shall say that which is written after the said Sentences.

WHEN the wicked man turneth away from his wickedness that he hath committed, and doeth that which is lawful and right, he shall save his soul alive. *Ezek.* xviii. 27.

The sacrifices of God are a broken spirit: a broken and a contrite heart, O God, thou wilt not despise. *Psal.* li. 17.

To the Lord our God belong mercies and for-givenesses, though we have rebelled against him: neither have we obeyed the voice of the Lord our God, to walk in his laws which he set before us. *Dan.* ix. 9, 10.

I will arise, and go to my father, and will say unto him, Father, I have sinned against heaven and before thee, and am no more worthy to be called thy son. *Luke,* xv. 18, 19.

Enter not into judgment with thy servant, O Lord; for in thy sight shall no man living be justi-fied. *Psal.* cxliii. 2.

DEarly beloved brethren, the Scripture moveth us, in sundry places, to acknowledge and confess our manifold sins and wickedness; and that

we

we fhould not diffemble nor cloke them before the
face of Almighty God, our heavenly Father;
but confefs them with an humble, lowly, penitent, and obedient heart ; to the end that we may
obtain forgivenefs of the fame by his infinite
goodnefs and mercy. Wherefore I pray and befeech you, as many as are here prefent, to accompany me with a pure heart and humble voice,
unto the throne of the heavenly grace, faying
after me.

*A general Confeffion to be faid of the whole Congrega-
tion, after the Minifter; all kneeling.*

ALmighty and moft merciful Father, We have
erred and ftrayed from thy ways like loft
fheep. We have followed too much the devices
and defires of our own hearts. We have offended
againft thy holy laws. We have left undone thofe
things which we ought to have done ; And we
have done thofe things which we ought not to have
done ; And there is no health in us. But thou,
O Lord, have mercy upon us, miferable offenders.
Spare thou them, O God, which confefs their
faults. Reftore thou them that are penitent ; According to thy promifes declared unto mankind in
Chrift Jefus our Lord. And grant, O moft merciful Father, for his fake ; That we may hereafter live a godly, righteous, and fober life ; To
the glory of thy holy Name. Amen.

Then the Minifter fhall fay,

O Lord, we befeech thee, abfolve thy people
from their offences ; that, through thy bountiful goodnefs, we may be delivered from the bands
of thofe fins, which by our frailty we have committed. Grant this, O heavenly Father, for
Jefus Chrift s fake, our bleffed Lord and Saviour.
Amen.

Then

Then the Minifter fhall fay the Lord's Prayer; the People alfo repeating it with him.

OUR Father which art in heaven, Hallowed be thy Name; Thy kingdom come; Thy will be done in earth, as it is in heaven: Give us this day our daily bread; And forgive us our trefpaffes, as we forgive them that trefpafs againft us: And lead us not into temptation; But deliver us from evil: For thine is the Kingdom, and the Power, and the Glory, For ever and ever.   Amen.

Then likewife he fhall fay,

O Lord, open thou our lips,

Anfw. And our mouth fhall fhew forth thy praife.

Minifter. O God make fpeed to fave us.

Anfw. O Lord make hafte to help us.

Here all ftanding up the Minifter fhall fay,

Glory be to the Father, and to the Son: and to the Holy Ghoft;

Anfw. As it was in the beginning, is now, and ever fhall be: world without end.   Amen.

Minifter. Praife ye the Lord.

Anfw. The Lord's Name be praifed.

Then fhall be faid the Pfalms in order as they are appointed. Then a Leffon of the Old Teftament, as is appointed: And after that the following Pfalm:

O Sing unto the Lord a new fong: for he hath done marvellous things.

With his own right hand, and with his holy arm; hath he gotten himfelf the victory.

The Lord declared his falvation: his righteouf-nefs hath he openly fhewed in the fight of the heathen.

He

He hath remembered his mercy and truth towards the houfe of Ifrael ; and all the ends of the world have feen the falvation of our God.

Shew yourfelves joyful unto the Lord, all ye lands : fing, rejoice, and give thanks.

Let the fea make a noife, and all that therein is; the round world and they that dwell therein.

Let the floods clap their hands, and let the hills be joyful together before the Lord : for he cometh to judge the earth.

With righteoufnefs fhall he judge the world ; and the people with equity.

Glory be to the Father, &c.

As it was in the beginning, &c.

Then a Leſſon of the New Teſtament, as it is appointed: And after that the following Pſalm :

GOD be merciful unto us, and blefs us ; and fhew us the light of his countenance, and be merciful unto us.

That thy way may be known upon earth ; thy faving health among all nations.

Let the people praife thee, O God : yea, let all the people praife thee.

O let the nations rejoice and be glad ; for thou fhalt judge the folk righteoufly, and govern the nations upon earth.

Let the people praife thee, O God : yea, let all the people praife thee.

Then fhall the earth bring forth her increafe ; and God, even our own God, fhall give us his bleffing.

God fhall blefs us : and all the ends of the world fhall fear him.

Glory be to the Father, &c.

As it was in the beginning, &c.

Then

Then shall be said the Apostles Creed by the Minister
and the People ; standing.

I Believe in God the Father Almighty, Maker of
Heaven and Earth :

And in Jesus Christ his only Son our Lord ; Who
was conceived by the Holy Ghost ; Born of the Virgin Mary ; Suffered under Pontius Pilate ; Was crucified, dead, and buried, He descended into hell :
The third day he rose again from the dead ;
He ascended into heaven, and sitteth on the right
hand of God the Father Almighty ; From thence
he shall come to judge the quick and the dead.

I believe in the Holy Ghost ; the Holy Catholic
Church, the Communion of Saints ; The forgiveness of sins ; The resurrection of the body ;
And the life everlasting.   Amen.

Then shall the Minister pronounce with a loud Voice,
The Lord be with you.
Answ. And with thy spirit.
Minist. Let us pray.
Lord, have mercy upon us.
Answ. Christ, have mercy upon us.
Minist. Lord, have mercy upon us.

Then shall follow three Collects ; the first of the Day ;
the second for Peace, the third for aid against all
Perils.

The second Collect at Evening-Prayer.

O God, from whom all holy desires, all good
counsels, and all just works do proceed ; Give
unto thy servants that peace which the world cannot give ; that both our hearts may be set to obey
thy commandments, and also that by thee we
being defended from the fear of our enemies, may
pass our time in rest and quietness, through the
merits of Jesus Christ our Saviour. *Amen.*

The

The third Collect, for Aid against all Perils.

Lighten our darknefs, we befeech thee, O Lord; and by thy great mercy defend us from all perils and dangers of this night, for the love of thy only Son our Saviour Jefus Chrift. *Amen.*

A Prayer for the Supreme Rulers.

O Lord our heavenly Father, high and mighty, King of kings, Lord of lords, the only Ruler of princes, who doft from thy throne behold all the dwellers upon earth; Moft heartily we befeech thee, with thy favour to behold the Supreme Rulers of thefe United States; and fo replenifh them with the grace of thy Holy Spirit, that they may incline to thy will, and walk in thy way; through Jefus Chrift our Lord. *Amen.*

Almighty God, who haft given us grace, at this time, with one accord to make our common fupplications unto thee; and doft promife, that when two or three are gathered together in thy Name, thou wilt grant their requefts; Fulfil now, O Lord, the defires and petitions of thy Servants, as may be moft expedient for them; granting us in this world knowledge of thy truth, and in the world to come life everlafting. *Amen.*

2 Cor. xiii. 14.

THE grace of our Lord Jefus Chrift, and the love of God, and the fellowfhip of the Holy Ghoft, be with you all evermore. *Amen.*

Here endeth the Order of Evening Prayer.

Here

Here followeth the LITANY, or General Supplication, to be said upon Wednesdays *and* Fridays.

O God the Father of heaven ; have mercy upon us miserable sinners.

O God the Father of heaven; have mercy upon us miserable sinners.

O God the Son, Redeemer of the world ; have mercy upon us miserable sinners.

O God the Son, Redeemer of the world ; have mercy upon us miserable sinners.

O God the Holy Ghost, proceeding from the Father and the Son ; have mercy upon us miserable sinners.

O God the Holy Ghost, proceeding from the Father and the Son ; have mercy upon us miserable sinners.

O holy, blessed, and glorious Trinity, three persons, and one God ; have mercy upon us miserable sinners.

O holy, blessed, and glorious Trinity, three persons, and one God ; have mercy upon us miserable sinners.

Remember not, Lord, our offences, nor the offences of our forefathers ; neither take thou vengeance of our sins : spare us, good Lord, spare thy people, whom thou hast redeemed with thy most precious blood, and be not angry with us for ever.

Spare us, good Lord.

From all evil and mischief ; from sin, from the crafts and assaults of the devil, from thy wrath, and from everlasting damnation,

Good Lord, deliver us.

From all blindness of heart ; from pride, vainglory, and hypocrisy ; from envy, hatred, and malice, and all uncharitableness,

Good Lord, deliver us.

From

From fornication, and all other deadly fin; and from all the deceits of the world, the flefh, and the devil,

Good Lord, deliver us.

From lightning and tempeft; from plague, peftilence, and famine; from battle and murder, and from fudden death,

Good Lord, deliver us.

From all fedition, privy confpiracy, and rebellion; from all falfe doctrine, herefy and fchifm; from hardnefs of heart, and contempt of thy word and commandment,

Good Lord, deliver us.

By the myftery of thy holy Incarnation; by thy holy Nativity and Circumcifion; by thy Baptifm, Fafting, and Temptation,

Good Lord, deliver us.

By thine Agony and bloody Sweat; by thy Crofs and Paffion; by thy precious Death and Burial; by thy glorious Refurrection and Afcenfion; and by the coming of the Holy Ghoft,

Good Lord, deliver us.

In all time of our tribulation; in all time of our wealth; in the hour of death, and in the day of judgment,

Good Lord, deliver us.

We finners do befeech thee to hear us, O Lord God, and that it may pleafe thee to rule and govern thy holy Church univerfal in the right way;

We befeech thee to hear us, good Lord.

That it may pleafe thee to keep and ftrengthen in the true worfhipping of thee, in righteoufnefs and holinefs of life, thy fervants the Supreme Rulers of thefe United States;

We befeech thee to hear us, good Lord.

That it may pleafe thee to rule their hearts in thy faith, fear, and love, that they may evermore

have

have affiance in thee, and ever seek thy honour
and glory;
We beseech thee to hear us, good Lord.

That it may please thee to illuminate all the
Ministers of thy Gospel, with true knowledge and
understanding of thy Word: that both by their
preaching and living they may set it forth, and shew
it accordingly;
We beseech thee to hear us, good Lord.

That it may please thee to bless and keep the
Magistrates, giving them grace to execute justice,
and to maintain truth;
We beseech thee to hear us, good Lord.

That it may please thee to bless and keep all thy
people;
We beseech thee to hear us, good Lord.

That it may please thee to give to all nations
unity, peace and concord;
We beseech thee to hear us, good Lord.

That it may please thee to give us an heart to
love and dread thee, and diligently to live after
thy commandments;
We beseech thee to hear us, good Lord.

That it may please thee to give to all thy people
increase of grace, to hear meekly thy Word, and
to receive it with pure affection, and to bring forth
the fruits of the Spirit;
We beseech thee to hear us, good Lord.

That it may please thee to bring into the way of
truth all such as have erred, and are deceived;
We beseech thee to hear us, good Lord.

That it may please thee to strengthen such as do
stand, and to comfort and help the weak-hearted,
and to raise up them that fall, and finally to beat
down Satan under our feet;
We beseech thee to hear us, good Lord.

That it may please thee to succour, help, and
comfort

comfort all that are in danger, neceffity, and tribulation ;

    We befeech thee to hear us, good Lord.

That it may pleafe thee to preferve all that travel
by land or by water, all women labouring with
child, all fick perfons and young children, and to
fhew thy pity upon all prifoners and captives ;

    We befeech thee to hear us, good Lord.

That it may pleafe thee to defend, and provide
for, the fatherlefs children, and widows, and all
that are defolate and oppreffed;

    We befeech thee to hear us, good Lord.

That it may pleafe thee to have mercy upon all
men ;

    We befeech thee to hear us, good Lord.

That it may pleafe thee to forgive our enemies,
perfecutors, and flanderers, and to turn their
hearts ;

    We befeech thee to hear us, good Lord.

That it may pleafe thee to give and preferve to
our ufe the kindly fruits of the earth, fo as in due
time we may enjoy them ;

    We befeech thee to hear us, good Lord.

That it may pleafe thee to give us true re-
pentance, to forgive us all our fins, negligences,
and ignorances, and to endue us with the grace of
thy Holy Spirit, to amend our lives according to
thy holy Word;

    We befeech thee to hear us, good Lord.

Son of God : we befeech thee to hear us.

    Son of God: we befeech thee to hear us.

O Lamb of God, that takeft away the fins of
the world;

    Grant us thy peace.

O Lamb of God, that takeft away the fins of
the world ;

    Have mercy upon us.

                        O Chrift,

O Chrift, hear us.

O Chrift, hear us.

Lord, have mercy upon us.

Lord, have mercy upon us.

Chrift, have mercy upon us.

Chrift, have mercy upon us.

  Lord, have mercy upon us.

  Lord, have mercy upon us.

Then fhall the Minifter and the People with him, fay the Lord's Prayer.

OUR Father, who art in Heaven, Hallowed be thy Name; Thy Kingdom come; Thy will be done on earth, as it is in heaven; Give us this day our daily bread; And forgive us our trefpaffes, as we forgive them that trefpafs againft us; And lead us not into Temptation, but deliver us from evil. Amen.

Minifter. O Lord, deal not with us after our fins :

Anfwer. Neither reward us after our iniquities.

Let us pray.

O God, merciful Father, that defpifeft not the fighing of a contrite heart, nor the defire of fuch as be forrowful; Mercifully affift our prayers that we make before thee, in all our troubles and adverfities whenfoever they opprefs us; and gracioufly hear us, that thofe evils, which the craft and fubtilty of the devil or man worketh againft us, be brought to nought, and by the providence of thy goodnefs be difperfed; that we thy fervants, being hurt by no perfecutions, may evermore give thanks unto thee in thy holy Church, through Jefus Chrift our Lord.

O Lord, arife, help us, and deliver us for thy Name's fake.

O God,

O God, we have heard with our Ears, and our
fathers have declared unto us the noble works
that thou didſt in their days, and in the old time
before them.

*O Lord, ariſe, help us, and deliver us for thine
honour.*

Glory be to the Father, and to the Son, and to
the Holy Ghoſt.

Anſw. As it was in the beginning, is now, and
ever ſhall be, world without end. Amen.

From our enemies defend us, O Chriſt.

Graciouſly look upon our afflictions.

Pitifully behold the ſorrows of our hearts.

Mercifully forgive the ſins of thy people.

Favourably with mercy hear our prayers.

O Son of David, have mercy upon us.

Both now and ever vouchſafe to hear us, O
Chriſt.

*Graciouſly hear us, O Chriſt ; graciouſly hear us,
O Lord Chriſt.*

O Lord, let thy mercy be ſhewed upon us ;
As we do put our truſt in thee.

Let us pray.

WE humbly beſeech thee, O Father, mercifully
to look upon our infirmities ; and, for the
glory of thy Name, turn from us all thoſe evils that
we moſt righteouſly have deſerved ; and grant that
in all our troubles we may put our whole truſt and
confidence in thy mercy, and evermore ſerve thee
in holineſs and pureneſs of living, to thy honour
and glory, through our only Mediator and Advocate, Jeſus Chriſt our Lord. *Amen.*

ALmighty God, who haſt given us grace at this
time with one accord to make our common
ſupplications unto thee, and doſt promiſe that when
two or three are gathered together in thy Name,
thou wilt grant their requeſts ; fulfil now, O Lord,

B   the

the defires and petitions of thy fervants, as may be moft expedient for them : granting us in this world knowledge of thy truth, and in the world to come life everlafting. *Amen.*

2 *Cor.* xiii. 14.

THE grace of our Lord, Jefus Chrift, and the love of God, and the fellowfhip of the Holy Ghoft, be with you all evermore. *Amen.*

Here endeth the LITANY.

A PRAYER *and* THANKSGIVING,
to be ufed every Lord's Day.

O God, the Creator and Preferver of all man-kind, we humbly befeech thee for all forts and conditions of men, that thou wouldeft be pleafed to make thy ways known unto them, thy faving health unto all nations. More efpecially we pray for the good eftate of the Catholic Church ; that it may be fo guided and governed by thy good Spirit, that all who profefs and call themfelves Chriftians may be led into the way of truth, and hold the faith in unity of fpirit, in the bond of peace, and in righteoufnefs of life. Fi-nally, we commend to thy fatherly goodnefs, all thofe who are any ways afflicted or dif-treffed in mind, body, or eftate [* *efpe-cially thofe for whom our prayers are de-fired*]; that it may pleafe thee to comfort and relieve them according to their feveral neceffities ; giving them patience under their fufferings, and a happy iffue out of all their afflictions : and this we beg for Jefus Chrift's fake. *Amen.*

* *This to be faid when any defire the prayers of the Congrega-tion.*

Almighty

ALmighty God, Father of all mercies, we thine unworthy fervants do give thee moft humble and hearty thanks for all thy goodnefs and loving-kindnefs to us and to all men;

[*particularly to thofe who defire now to offer up their praifes and thankfgivings for thy late mercies vouchfafed unto them.*] We blefs thee for our creation, prefervation, and all the bleffings of this

* This to be faid when any that have been prayed for defire to return praife.

life; but above all, for thine ineftimable love in the redemption of the world by our Lord Jefus Chrift; for the means of grace, and for the hope of glory. And we befeech thee, give us that due fenfe of all thy mercies, that our hearts may be unfeignedly thankful, and that we may fhew forth thy praife not only with our lips, but in our lives, by giving up ourfelves to thy fervice, and by walking before thee in holinefs and righteoufnefs all our days, through Jefus Chrift our Lord, to whom with thee and the Holy Ghoft, be all honour and glory, world without end. *Amen.*

THE

COLLECTS, EPISTLES, and GOSPELS,
To be ufed throughout the Year.

The Firft Sunday in Advent.

The Colleƈt.

ALmighty God, give us grace that we may caft away the works of darknefs, and put upon us the armour of light, now in the time of

Note: Pages 27-124 are Wesley's arrangement of these propers.

B 2

The Order for the Adminiftration of the Lord's Supper.

The Table at the Communion-time, having a fair white Linen Cloth upon it, fhall ftand where Morning and Evening Prayers are appointed to be faid. And the Elder, ftanding at the Table, fhall fay the Lord's Prayer, with the Collect following, the People kneeling.

OUR Father, who art in Heaven, Hallowed be thy Name; Thy Kingdom come; Thy will be done on earth, as it is in heaven; Give us this day our daily bread; And forgive us our trefpaffes, as we forgive them that trefpafs againft us; And lead us not into Temptation, but deliver us from evil. *Amen.*

The Collect.

A Lmighty God, unto whom all hearts be open, all defires known, and from whom no fecrets are hid; cleanfe the thoughts of our hearts by the infpiration of thy Holy Spirit, that we may perfectly love thee, and worthily magnify thy holy Name, through Chrift our Lord. *Amen.*

Then fhall the Elder, turning to the People, rehearfe diftinctly all the TEN COMMANDMENTS: *and the People ftill kneeling fhall, after every Commandment, afk God Mercy for their Tranfgreffion thereof for the Time paft, and Grace to keep the fame for the Time to come, as followeth:*

Minifter.

G O D fpake thefe words, and faid, I am the Lord thy God: Thou fhalt have none other gods but me.

People.

People. Lord, have mercy upon us, and incline our hearts to keep this law.

Minift. Thou fhalt not make to thyfelf any graven image, nor the likenefs of any thing that is in heaven above, or in the earth beneath, or in the water under the earth. Thou fhalt not bow down to them, nor worfhip them: for I the Lord thy God am a jealous God, and vifit the fins of the fathers upon the children, unto the third and fourth generation of them that hate me, and fhew mercy unto thoufands in them that love me, and keep my commandments.

People. Lord, have mercy upon us, and incline our hearts to keep this law.

Minift. Thou fhalt not take the Name of the Lord thy God in vain: for the Lord will not hold him guiltlefs that taketh his Name in vain.

People. Lord, have mercy upon us, and incline our hearts to keep this law.

Minift. Remember that thou keep holy the Sabbath-day. Six days fhalt thou labour, and do all that thou haft to do; but the feventh day is the Sabbath of the Lord thy God: in it thou fhalt do no manner of work, thou, and thy fon, and thy daughter, thy man-fervant, and thy maid-fervant, thy cattle, and the ftranger that is within thy gates. For in fix days the Lord made heaven and earth, the fea, and all that in them is, and refted the feventh day; wherefore the Lord bleffed the feventh day, and hallowed it.

People. Lord, have mercy upon us, and incline our hearts to keep this law.

Minift. Honour thy father and thy mother, that thy days may be long in the land which the Lord thy God giveth thee.

People. Lord, have mercy upon us, and incline our hearts to keep this law.

Minift.

Minift. Thou fhalt do no murder.

People. Lord, have mercy upon us, and incline our hearts to keep this law.

Minift. Thou fhalt not commit adultery.

People. Lord, have mercy upon us, and incline our hearts to keep this law.

Minift. Thou fhalt not fteal.

People. Lord, have mercy upon us, and incline our hearts to keep this law.

Minift. Thou fhalt not bear falfe witnefs againft thy neighbour.

People. Lord, have mercy upon us, and incline our hearts to keep this law.

Minift. Thou fhalt not covet thy neighbour's houfe, thou fhalt not covet thy neighbour's wife, nor his fervant, nor his maid, nor his ox, nor his afs, nor any thing that is his.

People. Lord, have mercy upon us, and write all thefe thy laws in our hearts, we befeech thee.

Then fhall follow this Collect.

Let us pray.

ALmighty and everlafting God, we are taught by thy holy word, that the hearts of the Princes of the earth are in thy rule and governance, and that thou doft difpofe and turn them as it feemeth beft to thy godly wifdom ; we humbly befeech thee fo to difpofe and govern the hearts of the Supreme Rulers of thefe United States, our Governors, that in all their thoughts, words, and works, they may ever feek thy honour and glory, and ftudy to preferve thy people committed to their charge, in wealth, peace, and godlinefs. Grant this, O merciful Father, for thy dear Son's fake, Jefus Chrift our Lord. *Amen.*

F 4   *Then*

*Then ſhall be ſaid the Collect of the day. And imme-
diately after the Collect, the Elder ſhall read the
Epiſtle, ſaying,* The Epiſtle [*or,* The Portion of
Scripture appointed for the Epiſtle] is written
in the —— Chapter of —— beginning at the
—— Verſe *And the Epiſtle ended, he ſhall ſay,*
Here endeth the Epiſtle. *Then ſhall he read the
Goſpel, (the People all ſtanding up) ſaying,* The
holy Goſpel is written in the —— Chapter of
—— beginning at the —— Verſe.

Then ſhall follow the Sermon.

Then ſhall the Elder ſay one or more of theſe Sentences.

LET your light ſo ſhine before men, that they
may ſee your good works, and glorify your
Father who is in heaven. *Matth.* v. 16.

Lay not up for yourſelves treaſures upon earth,
where moth and ruſt do corrupt, and where thieves
break through and ſteal: but lay up for yourſelves
treaſures in heaven, where neither moth nor ruſt
doth corrupt, and where thieves do not break
through nor ſteal. *Matth.* vi. 19, 20.

Whatſoever ye would that men ſhould do unto
you, even ſo do unto them; for this is the law and
the prophets. *Matth.* vii. 12.

Not every one that ſaith unto me, Lord, Lord,
ſhall enter into the kingdom of heaven; but he that
doeth the will of my Father who is in heaven.
Matth. vii. 21.

Zaccheus ſtood forth, and ſaid unto the Lord,
Behold, Lord, the half of my goods I give to the
poor; and if I have done any wrong to any man,
I reſtore him four-fold. *Luke,* xix. 8.

Who goeth a warfare at any time of his own
coſt? who planteth a vineyard, and eateth not of
the fruit thereof? or who feedeth a flock, and
cateth not of the milk of the flock? 1 *Cor.* ix. 7.
If

If we have fown unto you fpiritual things, is it a great matter if we fhall reap your worldly things? 1 *Cor.* ix. 11.

Do ye not know, that they who minifter about holy things, live of the facrifice? and they who wait at the altar, are partakers with the altar? Even fo hath the Lord alfo ordained, that they who preach the Gofpel, fhould live of the Gofpel. 1 *Cor.* ix. 13, 14.

He that foweth little, fhall reap little: and he that foweth plenteoufly, fhall reap plenteoufly. Let every man do according as he is difpofed in his heart; not grudgingly, or of neceffity: for God loveth a chearful giver. 2 *Cor.* ix. 6, 7.

Let him that is taught in the Word, minifter unto him that teacheth in all good things. Be not deceived, God is not mocked: for whatfoever a man foweth, that fhall he reap. *Gal.* vi. 6, 7.

While we have time, let us do good unto all men, and efpecially unto them that are of the houfhold of faith. *Gal.* vi. 10.

Godlinefs with contentment is great gain: for we brought nothing into the world, and it is certain we can carry nothing out. 1 *Tim.* vi. 6, 7.

Charge them who are rich in this world, that they be ready to give, and glad to diftribute, laying up in ftore for themfelves a good foundation againft the time to come, that they may attain eternal life. 1 *Tim.* vi. 17, 18, 19.

God is not unrighteous, that he will forget your works and labour that proceedeth of love; which love ye have fhewed for his Name's fake, who have miniftered unto the faints, and yet do minifter. *Heb.* vi. 10.

To do good, and to diftribute, forget not; for with fuch facrifices God is well pleafed. *Hebr.* xiii. 16.

Whofo

Whofo hath this world's good, and feeth his brother have need, and fhutteth up his compaffion from him, how dwelleth the love of God in him? *1 John,* iii. 17.

Be merciful after thy power : If thou haft much, give plenteoufly : If thou haft little, do thy diligence gladly to give of that little : for fo gathereft thou thyfelf a good reward in the day of neceffity. *Tob.* iv. 8, 9.

He that hath pity upon the poor, lendeth unto the Lord ; and look what he layeth out, it fhall be paid him again. *Prov.* xix. 17.

Bleffed is the man that provideth for the fick and needy : the Lord fhall deliver him in the time of trouble. *Pfal.* xli. 1.

While thefe Sentences are in reading, fome fit perfon appointed for that purpofe, fhall receive the alms for the poor, and other devotions of the people, in a decent Bafon, to be provided for that purpofe ; and then bring it to the Elder, who fhall place it upon the Table.

After which done, the Elder fhall fay,

Let us pray for the whole ftate of Chrift's Church militant here on earth.

ALmighty and everliving God, who, by thy holy Apoftle, haft taught us to make prayers and fupplications, and to give thanks for all men ; We humbly befeech thee moft mercifully [* to accept our alms and oblations, and] to receive thefe our prayers, which we offer unto thy Divine Majefty ; befeeching thee to infpire continually the univerfal Church with the fpirit of truth, unity, and concord : and grant that all they that do confefs thy holy Name, may agree in the truth of thy holy word, and live in unity and godly love. We befeech

* If there be no alms or oblations, then fhall the words [of accepting our alms and oblations] be left unfaid.

7   thee

thee alſo to ſave and defend all Chriſtian Kings, Princes, and Governors ; and eſpecially thy Servants the Supreme Rulers of theſe United States ; that under them we may be godly and quietly governed : and grant unto all that are put in authority under them, that they may truly and indifferently adminiſter juſtice, to the puniſhment of wickedneſs and vice, and to the maintenance of thy true religion and virtue. Give grace, O heavenly Father, to all the Miniſters of thy Goſpel, that they may both by their life and doctrine ſet forth thy true and lively word, and rightly and duly adminiſter thy holy Sacraments. And to all thy people give thy heavenly grace ; and eſpecially to this Congregation here preſent ; that with meek heart and due reverence they may hear and receive thy holy word, truly ſerving thee in holineſs and righteouſneſs all the days of their life. And we moſt humbly beſeech thee of thy goodneſs, O Lord, to comfort and ſuccour all them, who in this tranſitory life are in trouble, ſorrow, need, ſickneſs, or any other adverſity. And we alſo bleſs thy holy Name, for all thy ſervants departed this life in thy faith and fear ; beſeeching thee to give us grace ſo to follow their good examples, that with them we may be partakers of thy heavenly kingdom. Grant this, O Father, for Jeſus Chriſt's ſake, our only Mediator and Advocate. *Amen.*

Then ſhall the Elder ſay to them that come to receive the Holy Communion.

YE that do truly and earneſtly repent of your ſins, and are in love and charity with your neighbours, and intend to lead a new life, following the commandments of God, and walking from henceforth in his holy ways ; Draw near with faith, and take this holy Sacrament to your comfort ; and make your humble confeſſion to Almighty God, meekly kneeling upon your knees.

Then

Then shall this general Confession be made by the Mi-
nister in the Name of all those that are minded to
receive the Holy Communion, both he and all the
people kneeling humbly upon their knees, and saying,

ALmighty God, Father of our Lord Jesus Christ,
Maker of all things, Judge of all men; We
acknowledge and bewail our manifold sins and
wickedness, Which we from time to time most
grievously have committed, By thought, word, and
deed, against thy Divine Majesty, provoking most
justly thy wrath and indignation against us. We
do earnestly repent, and are heartily sorry for these
our misdoings; The remembrance of them is
grievous unto us. Have mercy upon us, have
mercy upon us, most merciful Father; For thy
Son our Lord Jesus Christ's sake, forgive us all that
is past; And grant, that we may ever hereafter
serve and please thee in newness of life, To the
honour and glory of thy Name, Through Jesus
Christ our Lord. *Amen.*

Then shall the Elder say,

O Almighty God, our heavenly Father, who of
thy great mercy hast promised forgiveness of
sins to all them that with hearty repentance and
true faith turn unto thee; Have mercy upon us;
pardon and deliver us from all our sins, confirm
and strengthen us in all goodness, and bring us to
everlasting life, through Jesus Christ our Lord.
Amen.

Then all standing, the Elder shall say.

Hear what comfortable words our Saviour Christ
faith unto all that truly turn to him:
COME unto me, all ye that are burdened and
heavy-laden, and I will refresh you. *Matth.*
xi. 28,

So

So God loved the world, that he gave his only-begotten Son, to the end that all that believe in him, fhould not perifh, but have everlafting life. *John* iii. 16.

Hear alfo what St. Paul faith :

This is a true faying, and worthy of all men to be received, That Chrift Jefus came into the world to fave finners. 1 *Tim.* i. 15.

Hear alfo what St. John faith :

If any man fin, we have an Advocate with the Father, Jefus Chrift the righteous : and he is the propitiation for our fins. 1 *John*, ii. 1, 2.

After which the Elder fhall proceed, faying,

Lift up your hearts.

Anfw. We lift them up unto the Lord.

Elder. Let us give thanks unto our Lord God.

Anfw. It is meet and right fo to do.

Then fhall the Elder fay,

IT is very meet, right, and our bounden duty, that we fhould at all times, and in all places, give thanks unto thee, O Lord, Holy Father †, Almighty, Everlafting God.

Here fhall follow the proper Preface, according to the Time, if there be any efpecially appointed; or elfe immediately fhall follow ;

THerefore with Angels and Archangels and with all the company of heaven, we laud and magnify thy glorious Name, evermore praifing thee, and faying, Holy, holy, holy, Lord God of hofts, heaven and earth are full of thy glory. Glory be to thee, O Lord moft high. Amen.

---

† *Thefe Words* [Holy Father] *muft be omitted on Trinity Sunday.*

Proper

Proper Prefaces.

Upon Christmas-day.

BEcause thou didst give Jesus Christ thine only Son to be born as at this time for us, who, by the operation of the Holy Ghost, was made very man, and that without spot of sin, to make us clean from all sin. Therefore with Angels, &c.

Upon Easter-day.

BUT chiefly we are bound to praise thee for the glorious Resurrection of thy Son Jesus Christ our Lord : for he is the very Paschal Lamb, which was offered for us, and hath taken away the sin of the world ; who by his death hath destroyed death, and by his rising to life again, hath restored to us everlasting life. Therefore with Angels, &c.

Upon Ascension-day.

THrough thy most dearly beloved Son, Jesus Christ our Lord; who, after his most glorious Resurrection, manifestly appeared to all his Apostles, and in their sight ascended up into heaven, to prepare a place for us ; that where he is, thither we might also ascend, and reign with him in glory. Therefore with angels, &c.

Upon Whitsunday.

THrough Jesus Christ our Lord ; according to whose most true promise the Holy Ghost came down, as at this time, from heaven with a sudden great sound, as it had been a mighty wind, in the likeness of fiery tongues, lighting upon the Apostles, to teach them, and to lead them to all truth ; giving them both the gift of divers languages, and also boldness, with fervent zeal, constantly to preach the Gospel unto all nations, whereby we have been

brought

brought out of darkneſs and error, into the clear light and true knowledge of thee, and of thy Son Jeſus Chriſt. Therefore with Angels, *&c.*

Upon the Feaſt of Trinity.

WHO art one God, one Lord ; not one only perſon, but three perſons in one ſubſtance. For that which we believe of the glory of the Father, the ſame we believe of the Son, and of the Holy Ghoſt, without any difference or inequality. Therefore with Angels, *&c.*

After each of which Prefaces ſhall immediately be ſaid,

THerefore with Angels and Archangels, and with all the company of heaven, we laud and magnify thy glorious Name, evermore praiſing thee, and ſaying, Holy, holy, holy, Lord God of hoſts, heaven and earth are full of thy glory. Glory be to thee, O Lord moſt high. *Amen.*

Then ſhall the Elder, kneeling down at the Table, ſay, in the Name of all them that ſhall receive the Communion, this Prayer following ; the People alſo kneeling.

WE do not preſume to come to this thy Table, O merciful Lord, truſting in our own right-eouſneſs, but in thy manifold and great mercies. We are not worthy ſo much as to gather up the crumbs under thy table. But thou art the ſame Lord, whoſe property is always to have mercy : Grant us therefore, gracious Lord, ſo to eat the fleſh of thy dear Son Jeſus Chriſt, and to drink his blood, that our ſinful bodies may be made clean by his body, and our ſouls waſhed through his moſt precious blood, and that we may evermore dwell in him, and he in us. *Amen.*

Then the Elder ſhall ſay the Prayer of Conſecration, as followeth :

ALmighty God, our heavenly Father, who, of thy tender mercy, didſt give thine only Son Jeſus Chriſt to ſuffer death upon the croſs for our

F 8   redemption ;

redemption; who made there (by his oblation of himself once offered) a full, perfect, and sufficient sacrifice, oblation, and satisfaction for the sins of the whole world; and did institute, and in his holy Gospel command us to continue, a perpetual memory of that his precious death until his coming again; hear us, O merciful Father, we most humbly beseech thee, and grant that we, receiving these thy creatures of bread and wine, according to thy Son our Saviour Jesus Christ's holy institution, in remembrance of his death and passion, may be partakers of his most blessed Body and Blood: who, in the same night that he was betrayed * took bread; and when he had given thanks, he brake it †; and gave it to his disciples, saying, Take, eat; ‡ this is my Body which is given for you; do this in remembrance of me. Likewise after Supper § he took the Cup; and when he had given thanks, he gave it to them, saying, Drink ye all of this; for this ‖ is my Blood of the New Testament, which is shed for you, and for many, for the remission of sins: Do this as oft as ye shall drink it, in remembrance of me. *Amen.*

* *Here the Elder is to take the Patten into his Hands:*

† *And here to break the Bread:*

‡ *And here to lay his Hand upon all the Bread.*

§ *Here he is to take the Cup into his Hand:*

‖ *And here to lay his Hand upon every Vessel (be it Chalice or Flaggon) in which there is any Wine to be consecrated.*

Then shall the Minister first receive the Communion in both kinds himself, and then proceed to deliver the same to the other Ministers in like manner, (if any be present) and after that to the People also, in order, into their Hands. And when he delivereth the Bread to any one, he shall say,

THE Body of our Lord Jesus Christ, which was given for thee, preserve thy body and soul unto everlasting life. Take and eat this in remembrance

brance that Chriſt died for thee, and feed on him
in thy heart by faith with thankſgiving.

*And the Miniſter that delivereth the Cup to any one
ſhall ſay,*

THE Blood of our Lord Jeſus Chriſt, which was
ſhed for thee, preſerve thy body and ſoul unto
everlaſting life. Drink this in remembrance that
Chriſt's Blood was ſhed for thee, and be thankful.

*If the conſecrated Bread or Wine be all ſpent before all
have communicated, the Elder may conſecrate more,
by repeating the Prayer of Conſecration.*

*When all have communicated, the Miniſter ſhall return
to the Lord's Table, and place upon it what remain-
eth of the conſecrated Elements, covering the ſame
with a fair Linen Cloth.*

*Then ſhall the Elder ſay the Lord's Prayer, the People
repeating after him every Petition.*

OUR Father who art in Heaven, Hallowed
be thy Name; Thy kingdom come; Thy
Will be done on Earth, As it is in Heaven: Give
us this day our daily bread ; And forgive us our
treſpaſſes, As we forgive them that treſpaſs againſt
us; And lead us not into temptation; But deliver
us from evil : For thine is the Kingdom, and the
Power, and the Glory, For ever and ever. *Amen.*

After which ſhall be ſaid as followeth :

O Lord and heavenly Father, we thy humble ſervants deſire thy Fatherly goodneſs mercifully
to accept this our ſacrifice of praiſe and thankſgiving; moſt humbly beſeeching thee to grant that,
by the merits and death of thy Son Jeſus Chriſt,
and through faith in his blood, we and all thy whole
Church may obtain remiſſion of our ſins, and all
other benefits of his paſſion. And here we offer
and

and prefent unto thee, O Lord, ourfelves, our fouls
and bodies, to be a reafonable, holy, and lively facrifice unto thee ; humbly befeeching thee that all
we who are paitakers of this holy Communion,
may be filled with thy grace and heavenly benediction. And although we be unworthy, through
our manifold fins, to offer unto thee any facrifice,
yet we befeech thee to accept this our bounden duty
and fervice; not weighing our merits, but pardon-
ing our offences, through Jefus Chrift our Lord ;
by whom, and with whom, in the unity of the
Holy Ghoft, all honour and glory be unto thee,
O Father Almighty, world without end. *Amen.*

Then fhall be faid,

GLory be to God on high, and on earth peace,
good-will towards men. We praife thee, we
blefs thee, we worfhip thee, we glorify thee, we
give thanks to thee for thy great glory, O Lord
God, heavenly king, God the Father Almighty.

O Lord, the only-begotten Son Jefu Chrift ; O
Lord God, Lamb of God, Son of the Father, that
takeft away the fins of the world, have mercy upon
us. Thou that takeft away the fins of the world,
have mercy upon us. Thou that takeft away the
fins of the world, receive our prayer. Thou that
fitteft at the right hand of God the Father, have
mercy upon us.

For thou only art holy, thou only art the Lord,
thou only, O Chrift, with the Holy Ghoft, art
moft high in the glory of God the Father. *Amen.*

*Then the Elder, if he fee it expedient, may put up an
Extempore Prayer ; and afterwards fhall let the
People depart with this Bleffing :*

MAY the peace of God, which paffeth all underftanding, keep your hearts and minds in
the knowledge and love of God, and of his Son
Jefus

Jefus Chrift our Lord ; and the blessing of God
Almighty, the Father, the Son, and the Holy
Ghoft, be amongft you, and remain with you
always. *Amen.*

The Ministration of Baptism of Infants.

*The Minifter coming to the Font, which is to be filled
with pure Water, fhall fay,*

DEarly beloved, forafmuch as all men are conceived and born in fin, and that our Saviour
Chrift faith, None can enter into the kingdom of
God, except he be regenerate and born anew of
water and of the Holy Ghoft ; I befeech you to
call upon God the Father, through our Lord Jefus
Chrift, that of his bounteous mercy he will grant
to *this Child* that thing which by nature *he* cannot
have ; that *he* may be baptized with water and the
Holy Ghoft, and received into Chrift's holy
Church, and be made a *lively member* of the fame.

Then fhall the Minifter fay,
Let us pray.

ALmighty and everlafting God, who of thy great
mercy didft fave Noah and his family in the
ark from perifhing by water ; and alfo didft fafely
lead the children of Ifrael, thy people, through the
Red Sea, figuring thereby thy holy Baptifm ; and
by the Baptifm of thy well-beloved Son Jefus Chrift
in the river Jordan, didft fanctify water to the
myftical wafhing away of fin, We befeech thee,
for thine infinite mercies, that thou wilt look upon
this Child ; wafh *him* and fanctify *him* with the
Holy Ghoft ; that *he* being delivered from thy
wrath,

wrath, may be received into the ark of Chrift's
Church; and being ftedfaft in faith, joyful through
hope, and rooted in charity, may fo pafs the
waves of this troublefome world, that finally *he*
may come to the land of everlafting life; there *to*
reign with thee, world without end, through Jefus
Chrift our Lord. *Amen.*

A Lmighty and immortal God, the aid of all that
need, the helper of all that flee to thee for
fuccour, the life of them that believe, and the refurrection of the dead, we call upon thee for *this
Infant*, that *he*, coming to thy holy Baptifm, may
receive remiffion of *his* fins by fpiritual regeneration. Receive *him*, O Lord, as thou haft promifed
by thy well-beloved Son, faying, Afk, and ye fhall
have; feek, and ye fhall find; knock, and it fhall
be opened unto you: So give now unto us that
afk; let us that feek find; open the gate unto us
that knock; that *this Infant* may enjoy the everlafting benediction of thy heavenly wafhing, and may
come to the eternal kingdom which thou haft promifed by Chrift our Lord. *Amen.*

*Then fhall the People ftand up; and the Minifter fhall
fay,*

Hear the words of the Gofpel written by Saint
Mark, in the Tenth Chapter, at the Thirteenth
Verfe.

T HEY brought young children to Chrift, that
he fhould touch them. And his difciples rebuked thofe that brought them; but when Jefus
faw it he was much difpleafed, and faid unto them,
Suffer the little children to come unto me, and for-
bid them not, for of fuch is the kingdom of God.
Verily, I fay unto you, Whofoever fhall not receive the kingdom of God as a little child, he fhall
not

not enter therein. And he took them up in his arms, put his hands upon them, and blessed them.

Then shall the Minister say,

ALmighty and everlasting God, heavenly Father, we give thee humble thanks, that thou hast vouchsafed to call us to the knowledge of thy grace, and faith in thee : Increase this knowledge, and confirm this faith in us evermore. Give thy Holy Spirit to *this Infant*, that *he* may be born again, and be made *an heir* of everlasting salvation, through our Lord Jesus Christ, who liveth and reigneth with thee and the Holy Spirit, now and for ever. *Amen.*

O Merciful God, grant that the old Adam in *this Child* may be so buried, that the new man may be raised up in *him.* *Amen.*

Grant that all carnal affections may die in *him,* and that all things belonging to the Spirit may live and grow in *him.* *Amen.*

Grant that *he* may have power and strength to have victory, and to triumph against the devil, the world, and the flesh. *Amen.*

Grant that whosoever is dedicated to thee by our office and ministry, may also be endued with heavenly virtues, and everlastingly rewarded, through thy mercy, O blessed Lord God, who dost live and govern all things, world without end. *Amen.*

ALmighty everliving God, whose most dearly beloved Son Jesus Christ, for the forgiveness of our sins, did shed out of his most precious side both water and blood ; and gave commandment to his disciples, that they should go teach all nations, and baptize them, in the Name of the Father, and of the Son, and of the Holy Ghost : Regard, we beseech thee, the supplications of thy congregation ; sanctify this water to the mystical washing away of

sin ;

fin; and grant that *this Child*, now to be baptized, may receive the fulnefs of thy grace, and ever remain in the number of thy faithful and elect children, through Jefus Chrift our Lord. *Amen.*

Then the Minifter fhall take the Child into his Hands, and fay to the Friends of the Child,

Name this Child.

And then, naming it after them, he fhall dip it in the Water, or fprinkle it therewith, faying,

N. I baptize thee, In the Name of the Father, and of the Son, and of the Holy Ghoft. *Amen.*

Then the Minifter fhall fay,

WE receive this Child into the Congregation of Chrift's flock, and * fign *him* with the fign of the Crofs; in token that hereafter *he* fhall not be afhamed to confefs the faith of Chrift crucified, and manfully to fight under his banner againft fin, the world and the devil; and to continue Chrift's faithful foldier and fervant unto his life's end. *Amen.*

* *Here the Minifter fhall make a Crofs upon the Child's Forehead.*

Then fhall the Minifter fay,

SEeing now, dearly beloved brethren, that *this Child is* grafted into the body of Chrift's Church, let us give thanks unto Almighty God for thefe benefits, and with one accord make our prayers unto him, that *this Child* may lead the reft of *his* life according to this beginning.

Then fhall be faid, all kneeling,

OUR Father, who art in heaven, Hallowed be thy Name; Thy kingdom come; Thy will be done on earth, as it is in heaven: Give us this day our daily bread; and forgive us our trefpaffes,

paffes, as we forgive them that trefpafs againft us; And lead us not into temptation; But deliver us from evil. *Amen.*

Then fhall the Minifter fay,

WE yield thee hearty thanks, moft merciful Father, that it hath pleafed thee to receive *this Infant* for thine own *Child* by adoption, and to incorporate *him* into thy holy Church. And humbly we befeech thee to grant, that *he,* being dead unto fin, and living unto righteoufnefs, and being buried with Chrift in his death, may crucify the old man, and utterly abolifh the whole body of fin; and that, as *he is* made *partaker* of the death of thy Son, *he* may alfo be *partaker* of his refurrection; fo that finally, with the refidue of thy holy Church, *he* may be *an inheritor* of thine everlafting kingdom, through Chrift our Lord. *Amen.*

The Miniftration of BAPTISM to fuch as are of RIPER YEARS.

The Minifter fhall fay,

DEarly beloved, forafmuch as all men are conceived and born in fin (and that which is born of the flefh is flefh, and they that are in the flefh cannot pleafe God, but live in fin, committing many actual tranfgreffions); and that our Saviour Chrift faith, None can enter into the kingdom of God, except he be regenerate and born anew of water and of the Holy Ghoft; I befeech you to call upon God the Father, through our Lord Jefus Chrift, that of his bounteous goodnefs he will grant to *thefe Perfons,* that which by nature *they* cannot have; that *they* may be baptized with Water and the Holy Ghoft, and received into Chrift's holy Church, and be made lively *members* of the fame.

Then

Then ſhall the Miniſter ſay,

Let us pray.

(And here all the Congregation ſhall kneel.)

ALmighty and everlaſting God, who of thy great mercy didſt ſave Noah and his family in the ark from periſhing by water; and alſo didſt ſafely lead the children of Iſrael thy people through the Red Sea, figuring thereby thy holy Baptiſm; and by the Baptiſm of thy well-beloved Son Jeſus Chriſt in the river Jordan, didſt ſanctify the element of water to the myſtical waſhing away of ſin; We beſeech thee, for thine infinite mercies, that thou wilt mercifully look upon *theſe* thy *Servants;* waſh *them* and ſanctify *them* with the Holy Ghoſt; that *they* being delivered from thy wrath, may be received into the ark of Chriſt's Church; and being ſtedfaſt in faith, joyful through hope, and rooted in charity, may ſo paſs the waves of this troubleſome world, that finally *they* may come to the land of everlaſting life; there to reign with thee, world without end, through Jeſus Chriſt our Lord. *Amen.*

ALmighty and immortal God, the aid of all that need, the helper of all that flee to thee for ſuccour, the life of them that believe, and the reſurrection of the dead; We call upon thee for *theſe Perſons;* that *they,* coming to thy holy Baptiſm, may receive remiſſion of *their* ſins by ſpiritual regeneration. Receive *them,* O Lord, as thou haſt promiſed by thy well beloved Son, ſaying, Aſk, and ye ſhall receive; ſeek, and ye ſhall find; knock, and it ſhall be opened unto you: So give now unto us that aſk; let us that ſeek find; open the gate unto us that knock; that *theſe Perſons* may enjoy the everlaſting benediction of thy heavenly waſhing, and may come to the eternal kingdom which thou haſt promiſed by Chriſt our Lord. *Amen.*

2

Then

*Then ſhall the People ſtand up, and the Miniſter ſhall
ſay,*

Hear the words of the Goſpel written by Saint *John*,
in the third Chapter, beginning at the firſt Verſe.

THERE was a man of the Phariſees, named Nicodemus, a ruler of the Jews: The ſame
came to Jeſus by night, and ſaid unto him, Rabbi,
we know that thou art a teacher come from God;
for no man can do theſe miracles that thou doeſt,
except God be with him. Jeſus anſwered and ſaid
unto him, Verily, verily, I ſay unto thee, Except a man be born again, he cannot ſee the
kingdom of God. Nicodemus ſaith unto him,
How can a man be born when he is old?
Can he enter the ſecond time into his mother's womb, and be born? Jeſus anſwered, Verily, verily, I ſay unto thee, Except a man be
born of water, and of the Spirit, he cannot enter
into the kingdom of God. That which is born
of the fleſh, is fleſh; and that which is born of the
Spirit, is ſpirit. Marvel not that I ſaid unto thee,
Ye muſt be born again. The wind bloweth
where it liſteth, and thou heareſt the ſound thereof; but canſt not tell whence it cometh, and
whither it goeth: ſo is every one that is born of
the Spirit.

After which he ſhall ſay,

ALmighty and everlaſting God, heavenly Father, we give thee humble thanks, for that
thou haſt vouchſafed to call us to the knowledge of thy grace, and faith in thee: Increaſe this knowledge, and confirm this faith in
us evermore. Give thy Holy Spirit to *theſe Perſons*,
that *they* may be born again, and be made *heirs*
of everlaſting ſalvation, through our Lord Jeſus

G   Chriſt,

Chrift, who liveth and reigneth with thee and the Holy Spirit, now and for ever. *Amen.*

Then the Minister shall speak to the Persons *to be baptized, on this wise:*

WELL beloved, who *are* come hither, defiring to receive holy Baptifm, *ye* have heard how the Congregation hath prayed, that our Lord Jefus Chrift would vouchfafe to receive you, and blefs you, to releafe you of your fins, to give you the kingdom of heaven, and everlafting life. And our Lord Jefus Chrift hath promifed in his holy word, to grant all thofe things that we have prayed for; which promife he for his part will moft furely keep and perform.

Wherefore, after this promife made by Chrift, *you* muft alfo faithfully for *your* part promife, in the prefence of this whole Congregation, that *you* will renounce the devil and all his works, and conftantly believe God's holy Word, and obediently keep his Commandments.

Then shall the Minister demand of each of the Perfons to be baptized, severally,

Quest. DOST thou renounce the devil and all his works, the vain pomp and glory of the world, with all covetous defires of the fame, and the carnal defires of the flefh, fo that thou wilt not follow, or be led by them?

Answ. I renounce them all.

Quest. DOST thou believe in God the Father Almighty, Maker of heaven and earth. And in Jefus Chrift his only begotten Son our Lord? And that he was conceived by the Holy Ghoft; born of the Virgin Mary; that he fuffered under Pontius Pilate, was crucified, dead, and buried;

buried ; that he went down into hell, and alfo did rife again the third day; that he afcended into heaven, and fitteth at the right hand of God the Father Almighty ; and from thence fhall come again, at the end of the world, to judge the quick and the dead ?

And doft thou believe in the Holy Ghoft ; the Holy Catholic Church ; the Communion of Saints ; the Remiffion of Sins ; the Refurrection of the Body ; and everlafting Life after Death ?

Anfw. All this I ftedfaftly believe.

Queft. WILT thou be baptized in this faith ?
Anfw. This is my defire.

Queft. WILT thou then obediently keep God's holy will and commandments, and walk in the fame all the days of thy life ?

Anfw. I will endeavour fo to do, God being my helper.

Then fhall the Minifter fay,

O Merciful God, grant that the old Adam in *thefe Perfons* may be fo buried, that the new man may be raifed up in *them. Amen.*

Grant that all carnal affections may die in *them,* and that all things belonging to the Spirit may live and grow in *them. Amen.*

Grant that *they* may have power and ftrength to have victory, and to triumph againft the devil, the world, and the flefh. *Amen.*

Grant that *they* being here dedicated to thee by our Office and Miniftry, may alfo be endued with heavenly virtues, and everlaftingly rewarded, through thy mercy, O bleffed Lord God, who doft live and govern all things, world without end. *Amen.*

G 2　　　　Almighty

ALmighty everliving God, whose most dearly beloved Son Jesus Christ, for the forgiveness of our sins, did shed out of his most precious side both water and blood; and gave commandment to his disciples, that they should go teach all nations, and baptize them, in the Name of the Father, and of the Son, and of the Holy Ghost: Regard, we beseech thee, the supplications of this congregation; sanctify this water to the mystical washing away of sin; and grant that the *Persons* now to be baptized, may receive the fulness of thy grace, and ever remain in the number of thy faithful and elect children, through Jesus Christ our Lord. *Amen.*

Then shall the Minister take each Person to be baptized by the Right Hand; and placing him conveniently by the Font, according to his Discretion, shall ask the Name; and then shall dip him in the Water, or pour Water upon him, saying,

N. I baptize thee, In the Name of the Father, and of the Son, and of the Holy Ghost. *Amen.*

Then shall the Minister say,

SEeing now, dearly beloved brethren, that *these Persons are* grafted into the body of Christ's Church; let us give thanks unto Almighty God for these benefits, and with one accord make our prayers unto him, that *they* may lead the rest of *their* life according to this beginning.

Then shall be said the Lord's Prayer, all kneeling.

OUR Father, who art in heaven, Hallowed be thy Name; Thy kingdom come; Thy will be done on earth, as it is in heaven: Give us this day our daily bread; and forgive us our trespasses, as we forgive them that trespass against us; And

And lead us not into temptation; But deliver us from evil. *Amen.*

WE yield thee humble thanks, O heavenly Father, that thou haft vouchfafed to call us to the knowledge of thy grace, and faith in thee; Increate this knowledge, and confirm this faith in us evermore. Give thy Holy Spirit to *thefe Perfons*; that being born again, and made *heirs* of everlafting falvation, through our Lord Jefus Chrift, *they* may continue thy *fervants*, and attain thy promifes, through the fame Lord Jefus Chrift thy Son; who liveth and reigneth with thee, in the unity of the fame Holy Spirit, everlaftingly. *Amen.*

The Form of Solemnization of MATRI-MONY.

Firft, the Banns of all that are to be married together, muft be publifhed in the Congregation, three feveral Sundays, in the Time of Divine Service; the Minifter faying after the accuftomed Manner,

I Publifh the Banns of Marriage between *M.* of —— and *N.* of ——. If any of you know caufe or juft impediment, why thefe two perfons fhould not be joined together in holy Matrimony, ye are to declare it: This is the firft [*fecond,* or *third*] time of afking.

At the Day and Time appointed for Solemnization of Matrimony, the Perfons to be married, ftanding together, the Man on the Right Hand, and the Woman on the Left, the Minifter fhall fay,

DEarly beloved, we are gathered together here in the fight of God, and in the face of this Congregation, to join together this Man and this

Woman

Woman in holy Matrimony ; which is an honourable eſtate, inſtituted of God in the time of man's innocency, ſignifying unto us the myſtical union that is betwixt Chriſt and his Church : which holy eſtate Chriſt adorned and beautified with his preſence, and firſt miracle that he wrought in Cana of Galilee, and is commended of St. Paul to be honourable among all men ; and therefore is not by any to be enterprized, or taken in hand unadviſedly, lightly or wantonly, to ſatisfy men's carnal luſts and appetites, like brute beaſts, that have no underſtanding ; but reverently, diſcreetly, adviſedly, ſoberly, and in the fear of God ; duly conſidering the cauſes for which Matrimony was ordained.

Firſt, It was ordained for the procreation of children, to be brought up in the fear and nurture of the Lord, and to the praiſe of his holy Name.

Secondly, It was ordained for a remedy againſt ſin, and to avoid fornication ; that ſuch perſons as have not the gift of continency, might marry, and keep themſelves undefiled members of Chriſt's body.

Thirdly, It was ordained for the mutual ſociety, help, and comfort, that the one ought to have of the other, both in proſperity and adverſity.

Into which holy eſtate theſe two perſons preſent come now to be joined. Therefore if any man can ſhew any juſt cauſe why they may not lawfully be joined together, let him now ſpeak, or elſe hereafter for ever hold his peace.

And alſo ſpeaking unto the Perſons that are to be married, he ſhall ſay,

I Require and charge you both (as you will anſwer at the dreadful day of judgment, when the ſecrets of all hearts ſhall be diſcloſed) that if either of you know any impediment why you may not be
lawfully

lawfully joined together in Matrimony, you do now confefs it. For be ye well affured, that fo many as are coupled together otherwife than God's Word doth allow, are not joined together by God, neither is their Matrimony lawful.

If no Impediment be alledged, then fhall the Minifter fay unto the Man,

M. WILT thou have this woman to thy wedded wife, to live together after God's ordinance, in the holy eftate of Matrimony? Wilt thou love her, comfort her, honour, and keep her, in ficknefs, and in health; and forfaking all other, keep thee only unto her, fo long as you both fhall live?

The Man fhall anfwer,
I will.

Then fhall the Minifter fay unto the Woman,

N. WILT thou have this Man to thy wedded Hufband, to live together after God's ordinance, in the holy eftate of Matrimony? Wilt thou obey him, ferve him, love, honour, and keep him, in ficknefs and in health; and forfaking all other, keep thee only unto him, fo long as you both fhall live?

The Woman fhall anfwer,
I will.

Then the Minifter fhall caufe the Man with his Right Hand to take the woman by her Right Hand, and to fay after him as followeth:

I *M.* take thee *N.* to be my wedded wife, to have and to hold, from this day forward, for better for worfe, for richer for poorer, in ficknefs, and in health, to love and to cherifh, till death us do part, according to God's holy ordinance; and thereto I plight thee my Faith.

G 4 *Then*

Then shall they loose their Hands, and the Woman with her Right Hand taking the Man by his Right Hand, shall likewise say after the Minister :

I N. take thee M. to be my wedded Husband, to have and to hold, from this day forward, for better for worse, for richer for poorer, in sickness and in health, to love, cherish, and to obey, till death us do part, according to God's holy ordinance ; and thereto I give thee my Faith.

Then the Minister shall say,

Let us pray.

O Eternal God, Creator and Preserver of all mankind, Giver of all spiritual grace, the Author of everlasting life; Send thy blessing upon these thy servants, this Man and this Woman, whom we bless in thy Name ; that as Isaac and Rebecca lived faithfully together, so these persons may surely perform and keep the vow and covenant betwixt them made, and may ever remain in perfect love and peace together, and live according to thy laws, through Jesus Christ our Lord. *Amen.*

Then shall the Minister join their Right Hands together, and say,

Those whom God hath joined together, let no man put asunder.

Then shall the Minister speak unto the People :

FOrasmuch as M. and N. have consented together in holy wedlock, and have witnessed the same before God and this company, and thereto have pledged their faith either to other, and have declared the same by joining of hands; I pronounce that they are Man and Wife together, In the Name of the Father, and of the Son, and of the Holy Ghost. *Amen.*

And

And the Minister shall add this blessing :

GOD the Father, God the Son, God the Holy Ghost, bless, preserve, and keep you; the Lord mercifully with his favour look upon you, and so fill you with all spiritual benediction and grace, that ye may so live together in this life, that in the world to come ye may have life everlasting. *Amen.*

Then the Minister shall say,

Lord, have mercy upon us.

Answ. Christ, have mercy upon us.

Minister. Lord, have mercy upon us.

OUR Father, who art in heaven, Hallowed be thy Name; thy kingdom come; Thy will be done on earth, as it is in heaven: Give us this day our daily bread; And forgive us our trespasses, as we forgive them that trespass against us: And lead us not into temptation; but deliver us from evil. *Amen.*

Minister. O Lord, save thy servant and thy handmaid.

Answer. And let them put their trust in thee.

Minister. O Lord, send them help from thy holy place;

Answer. And evermore defend them.

Minister. Be unto them a tower of strength,

Answer. From the face of their enemy.

Minister O Lord, hear our prayer;

Answer. And let our cry come unto thee.

Minister.

O God of Abraham, God of Isaac, God of Jacob, bless these thy servants, and sow the seed of eternal life in their hearts, that whatsoever in thy holy Word they shall profitably learn, they may in deed fulfil the same. Look, O Lord, mercifully upon them from heaven, and bless them.

And as thou didſt ſend thy bleſſing upon Abraham and Sarah, to their great comfort ; ſo vouchſafe to ſend thy bleſſing upon theſe thy ſervants; that they obeying thy will, and always being in ſafety under thy protection, may abide in thy love unto their lives end, through Jeſus Chriſt our Lord. *Amen.*

This Prayer next following ſhall be omitted, where the Woman is paſt child-bearing.

O Merciful Lord and heavenly Father, by whoſe gracious gift mankind is increaſed ; We beſeech thee, aſſiſt with thy bleſſing theſe two perſons, that they may both be fruitful in the procreation of children, and alſo live together ſo long in godly love and honeſty, that they may ſee their children chriſtianly and virtuouſly brought up, to thy praiſe and honour, through Jeſus Chriſt our Lord. *Amen.*

O God, who by thy mighty power haſt made all things of nothing, who alſo (after other things ſet in order) didſt appoint that out of man (created after thine own image and ſimilitude) woman ſhould take her beginning : and knitting them together, didſt teach that it ſhould never be lawful to put aſunder thoſe whom thou by Matrimony hadſt made one ; O God, who haſt conſecrated the ſtate of Matrimony to ſuch an excellent myſtery, that in it is ſignified and repreſented the ſpiritual marriage and unity betwixt Chriſt and his Church ; Look mercifully upon theſe thy ſervants, that both this man may love his wife, according to thy Word (as Chriſt did love his ſpouſe the Church, who gave himſelf for it, loving and cheriſhing it, even as his own fleſh), and alſo that this woman may be loving and amiable, faithful and obedient to her huſband : and in all quietneſs, ſobriety, and peace, be a follower of holy and godly matrons. O Lord, bleſs them both, and grant them

to

to inherit thy everlasting kingdom, through Jesus Christ our Lord. *Amen.*

Then shall the Minister say,

ALmighty God, who at the beginning did create our first parents, Adam and Eve, and did sanctify and join them together in marriage; Pour upon you the riches of his grace, sanctify and bless you, that ye may please him both in body and soul, and live together in holy love unto your lives end. *Amen.*

The COMMUNION of the SICK.

The Collect.

ALmighty, everliving God, maker of mankind, who dost correct those whom thou dost love, and chastise every one whom thou dost receive; we beseech thee to have mercy upon this thy servant visited with thine hand; and to grant that *he* may take *his* sickness patiently, and recover *his* bodily health, if it be thy gracious will; and whensoever *his* soul shall depart from the body, it may be without spot presented unto thee, through Jesus Christ our Lord. *Amen.*

The Epistle. Heb. xii. 5, 6.

MY son, despise not thou the chastening of the Lord, nor faint when thou art rebuked of him: for whom the Lord loveth he chasteneth, and scourgeth every son whom he receiveth.

The Gospel. John, v. 24.

VErily, verily, I say unto you, He that heareth my word, and believeth on him that sent me, hath everlasting life, and shall not come into condemnation; but is passed from death unto life.

After which the Elder ſhall proceed according to the form before preſcribed for the Holy Communion, be-ginning at theſe words [Ye that do truly, &c.]

At the time of the diſtribution of the Holy Sacrament, the Elder ſhall firſt receive the Communion him-ſelf, and after miniſter unto them that are appointed to communicate with the ſick, and laſt of all to the ſick perſon.

The Order for the BURIAL of the DEAD.

The Miniſter meeting the Corpſe, and going before it, ſhall ſay,

I Am the reſurrection and the life, ſaith the Lord: he that believeth in me, though he were dead, yet ſhall he live : and whoſoever liveth and believ-eth in me, ſhall never die. *John*, xi. 25, 26.

I Know that my Redeemer liveth, and that he ſhall ſtand at the latter day upon the earth. And though after my ſkin, worms deſtroy this body, yet in my fleſh ſhall I ſee God : whom I ſhall ſee for myſelf, and mine eyes ſhall behold, and not ano-ther. *Job.* xix. 25, 26, 27.

WE brought nothing into this world, and it is certain we can carry nothing out. The Lord gave, and the Lord hath taken away ; bleſſed be the Name of the Lord. 1 *Tim.* vi. 7. *Job*, i. 21.

Then ſhall be read, Pſal. xc.

L ORD, thou haſt been our refuge from one ge-neration to another.

Before the mountains were brought forth, or ever the earth and the world were made, thou art God from everlaſting, and world without end.

Thou turneſt man to deſtruction : again thou ſayeſt, Come again, ye children of men.

For

For a thoufand years in thy fight are but as yefterday; feeing that is paft, as a watch in the night.

As foon as thou fcattereft them, they are even as a fleep, and fade away fuddenly like the grafs.

In the morning it is green, and groweth up: but in the evening it is cut down, dried up, and withered.

For we confume away in thy difpleafure; and are afraid at thy wrathful indignation.

Thou haft fet our mifdeeds before thee, and our fecret fins in the light of thy countenance.

For when thou art angry, all our days are gone: we bring our years to an end, as it were a tale that is told.

The days of our age are threefcore years and ten; and though men be fo ftrong, that they come to fourfcore years, yet is their ftrength then but labour and forrow : fo foon paffeth it away, and we are gone.

But who regardeth the power of thy wrath : for even according to thy fear, fo is thy difpleafure.

So teach us to number our days, that we may apply our hearts unto wifdom.

Turn thee again, O Lord, at the laft, and be gracious unto thy fervants.

O fatisfy us with thy mercy, and that foon ; fo fhall we rejoice and be glad all the days of our life.

Comfort us again now after the time that thou haft plagued us, and for the years wherein we have fuffered adverfity.

Shew thy fervants thy work, and their children thy glory.

And the glorious majefty of the Lord our God be upon us : profper thou the work of our hands upon us, O profper thou our handy-work.

Glory be to the Father, and to the Son, and to the Holy Ghoft;

As

As it was in the beginning, is now, and ever ſhall be, world without end. *Amen.*

Then ſhall follow the Leſſon taken out of the fifteenth chapter of the firſt Epiſtle of Saint Paul to the Corinthians.

1 Cor. xv. 20.

NOW is Chriſt riſen from the dead, and become the firſt-fruits of them that ſlept For ſince by man came death, by man came alſo the reſurrection of the dead. For as in Adam all die, even ſo in Chriſt ſhall all be made alive. But every man in his own order; Chriſt the firſt-fruits; afterward they that are Chriſt's, at his coming. Then cometh the end when he ſhall have delivered up the kingdom to God even the Father; when he ſhall have put down all rule and all authority and power: for he muſt reign till he hath put all enemies under his feet. The laſt enemy that ſhall be deſtroyed is death: for he hath put all things under his feet. But when he ſaith all things are put under him, it is manifeſt that he is excepted who did put all things under him. And when all things ſhall be ſubdued unto him, then ſhall the Son alſo himſelf be ſubject unto him that put all things under him, that God may be all in all. Elſe what ſhall they do who are baptized for the dead, if the dead riſe not at all? Why are they then baptized for the dead? and why ſtand we in jeopardy every hour? I proteſt by your rejoicing, which I have in Chriſt Jeſus our Lord, I die daily. If after the manner of men I have fought with beaſts at Epheſus, what advantageth it me, if the dead riſe not? Let us eat and drink for tomorrow we die. Be not deceived: evil communications corrupt good manners. Awake to righteouſneſs, and ſin not: for ſome have not the knowledge of God. I ſpeak this to your ſhame. But ſome man will ſay, How are the dead raiſed
up?

up? and with what body do they come? Thou fool, that which thou foweft is not quickened, except it die. And that which thou foweft, thou foweft not that body that fhall be, but bare grain, it may chance of wheat, or of fome other grain: But God giveth it a body as it hath pleafed him, and to every feed his own body. All flefh is not the fame flefh: but there is one kind of flefh of men, another flefh of beafts, another of fifhes, and another of birds. There are alfo celeftial bodies, and bodies terreftrial: but the glory of the celeftial is one, and the glory of the terreftrial is another. There is one glory of the fun, and another glory of the moon, and another glory of the ftars: for one ftar differeth from another ftar in glory. So alfo is the refurrection of the dead. It is fown in corruption; it is raifed in incorruption: it is fown in difhonour, it is raifed in glory: it is fown in weaknefs; it is raifed in power: it is fown a natural body, it is raifed a fpiritual body. There is a natural body, and there is a fpiritual body. And fo it is written, The firft man Adam was made a living foul; the laft Adam was made a quickening fpirit. Howbeit that was not firft which is fpiritual, but that which is natural; and afterward that which is fpiritual. The firft man is of the earth, earthy; the fecond man is the Lord from heaven. As is the earthy, fuch are they that are earthy: and as is the heavenly, fuch are they alfo that are heavenly. And as we have borne the image of the earthy, we fhall alfo bear the image of the heavenly. Now this I fay, brethren, that flefh and blood cannot inherit the kingdom of God; neither doth corruption inherit incorruption. Behold, I fhew you a myftery; We fhall not all fleep, but we fhall all be changed, in a moment, in the twinkling of an eye, at the laft trump: For the trumpet fhall found, and the dead fhall be raifed

I   incorruptible,

incorruptible, and we fhall be changed. For this corruptible muft put on incorruption, and this mortal muft put on immortality. So when this corruptible fhall have put on incorruption, and this mortal fhall have put on immortality, then fhall be brought to pafs the faying that is written. Death is fwallowed up in victory. O death, where is thy fting? O grave, where is thy victory? The fting of death is fin, and the ftrength of fin is the law. But thanks be to God, who giveth us the victory, through our Lord Jefus Chrift. Therefore, my beloved brethren, be ye ftedfaft, immoveable, always abounding in the work of the Lord; forafmuch as ye know that your labour is not in vain in the Lord.

At the Grave, when the Corpfe is laid in the earth, the Minifter fhall fay,

MAN that is born of a woman hath but a fhort time to live, and is full of mifery. He cometh up, and is cut down like a flower; he fleeth as it were a fhadow, and never continueth in one ftay.

In the midft of life we are in death; of whom may we feek for fuccour, but of thee, O Lord, who for our fins art juftly difpleafed?

Yet, O Lord God moft holy, O Lord moft mighty, O holy and moft merciful Saviour, deliver us not into the bitter pains of eternal death.

Thou knoweft, Lord, the fecrets of our hearts: fhut not thy merciful ears to our prayers; but fpare us, Lord moft holy, O God moft mighty, O holy and merciful Saviour, thou moft worthy Judge eternal, fuffer us not at our laft hour for any pains of death to fall from thee.

Then fhall be faid,

I Heard a voice from heaven, faying unto me, Write; From henceforth bleffed are the dead who die in the Lord: even fo faith the Spirit; for they reft from their labours.

2   *Then*

Then shall the Minister say,

Lord, have mercy upon us.

Chrift, have mercy upon us.

Lord, have mercy upon us.

OUR Father, who art in heaven, Hallowed be thy Name; Thy kingdom come; Thy will be done on earth, as it is in heaven : Give us this day our daily bread ; And forgive us our trefpaffes, as we forgive them that trefpafs againft us ; And lead us not into temptation ; But deliver us from evil. *Amen.*

The Collect.

O Merciful God, the Father of our Lord Jefus Chrift, who is the refurrection and the life ; in whom whofoever believeth fhall live, though he die : and whofoever liveth and believeth in him, fhall not die eternally : We meekly befeech thee, O Father, to raife us from the death of fin unto the life of righteoufnefs ; that when we fhall de- part this life, we may reft in him ; and at the ge- neral refurrection on the laft day, may be found acceptable in thy fight, and receive that bleffing which thy well–beloved Son fhall then pronounce to all that love and fear thee, faying, Come, ye bleffed children of my Father, receive the kingdom prepared for you from the beginning of the world. Grant this, we befeech thee, O merciful Father, through Jefus Chrift our Mediator and Redeemer. *Amen.*

THE grace of our Lord Jefus Chrift, and the love of God, and the fellowfhip of the Holy Ghoft, be with us all evermore. *Amen.*

SELECT

Note: Pages 162-279 are Wesley's "SELECT PSALMS."

The Form and Manner of Making and Ordaining of SUPERINTENDANTS, ELDERS, and DEACONS.

The Form and Manner of making of DEACONS.

When the Day appointed by the Superintendant is come, after Morning Prayer is ended, there shall be a Sermon, or Exhortation, declaring the Duty and Office of such as come to be admitted Deacons.

After which one of the Elders shall present unto the Superintendant the Persons to be ordained Deacons : and their Names being read aloud, the Superintendant shall say unto the People :

BRethren, if there be any of you, who knoweth any impediment or crime in any of these persons presented to be ordained deacons, for the which he ought not to be admitted to that office, let him come forth in the Name of God, and shew what the crime or impediment is.

And if any Crime or Impediment be objected, the Superintendant shall surcease from ordaining that Person, until such Time as the Party accused shall be found clear of that Crime.

Then the Superintendant (commending such as shall be found meet to be ordained, to the Prayers of the Congregation) shall, with the Ministers and People present, say the Litany.

Then

Then shall be said the Service for the Communion, with the Collect, Epistle, and Gospel, as followeth.

The Collect.

ALmighty God, who by thy Divine Providence haft appointed divers orders of minifters in thy church, and didft infpire thine apoftles to choofe into the order of deacons the firft martyr Saint Stephen, with others ; Mercifully behold thefe thy fervants now called to the like office and adminiftration ; replenifh them fo with the truth of thy doctrine, and adorn them with innocency of life, that both by word and good example they may faithfully ferve thee in this office, to the glory of thy Name, and the edification of thy church, through the merits of our Saviour Jefus Chrift, who liveth and reigneth with thee and the Holy Ghoft, now and for ever. *Amen.*

The Epiftle. 1 Tim. iii. 8.

LIkewife muft the Deacons be grave, not doubletongued, not given to much wine, not greedy of filthy lucre ; holding the myftery of the faith in a pure confcience. And let thefe alfo firft be proved ; then let them ufe the office of a deacon, being found blamelefs. Even fo muft their wives be grave, not flanderers, fober, faithful in all things. Let the deacons be the hufbands of one wife, ruling their children and their own houfes well. For they that have ufed the office of a deacon well, purchafe to themfelves a good degree, and great boldnefs in the faith which is in Chrift Jefus.

Then

Then shall the Superintendant examine every one of them that are to be ordained, in the Presence of the People, after this manner following :

DO you trust that you are inwardly moved by the Holy Ghost to take upon you this office and ministration, to serve God for the promoting of his glory, and the edifying of his people ?

Answer. I trust so.

The Superintendant.

DO you think that you are truly called, according to the will of our Lord Jesus Christ, to the ministry of the church ?

Answer. I think so.

The Superintendant.

DO you unfeignedly believe all the canonical Scriptures of the Old and New Testament ?

Answer. I do believe them.

The Superintendant.

WILL you diligently read the same unto the people whom you shall be appointed to serve ?

Answer. I will.

The Superintendant.

IT appertaineth to the office of a Deacon, to assist the elder in Divine Service, and especially when he ministereth the holy Communion, to help him in the distribution thereof, and to read and expound the holy Scriptures; to instruct the youth, and in the absence of the elder to baptize.   And furthermore, it is his office, to search for the sick, poor,
and

and impotent, that they may be vifited and relieved. Will you do this gladly and willingly?

Anfwer. I will do fo, by the help of God.

The Superintendant.

WILL you apply all your diligence to frame and fafhion your own lives, and the lives of your families, according to the doctrine of Chrift; and to make both yourfelves and them, as much as in you lieth, wholfome examples of the flock of Chrift?

Anfwer. I will fo do, the Lord being my helper.

The Superintendant.

WILL you reverently obey them to whom the charge and government over you is committed, following with a glad mind and will their godly admonitions?

Anfwer. I will endeavour fo to do, the Lord being my helper.

Then the Superintendant laying his Hands feverally upon the Head of every one of them fhall fay,

TAKE thou authority to execute the office of a deacon in the church of God; In the Name of the Father, and of the Son, and of the Holy Ghoft. *Amen.*

Then fhall the Superintendant deliver to every one of them the Holy Bible, faying,

TAKE thou authority to read the holy Scriptures in the church of God, and to preach the fame.

Then

Then one of them appointed by the Superintendant
shall read,

The Gospel. Luke, xii. 35.

LET your loins be girded about, and your lights
burning, and ye yourselves like unto men that
wait for their Lord, when he will return from the
wedding, that when he cometh and knocketh,
they may open unto him immediately. Blessed are
those servants, whom the Lord when he cometh
shall find watching. Verily I say unto you, That
he shall gird himself, and make them to sit down to
meat, and will come forth and serve them. And
if he shall come in the second watch, or come in
the third watch, and find them so, blessed are those
servants.

Then shall the Superintendant proceed in the Commu
nion, and all that are ordained shall receive the holy
Communion.

The Communion ended, immediately before the Bene-
diction, shall be said these Collects following :

ALmighty God, giver of all good things, who
of thy great goodness hast vouchsafed to accept and take these thy servants into the office of
deacons in thy church ; Make them, we beseech
thee, O Lord, to be modest, humble, and constant in their ministration, and to have a ready
will to observe all spiritual discipline ; that they
having always the testimony of a good conscience,
and continuing ever stable and strong in thy Son
Christ, may so well behave themselves in this in-
ferior office, that they may be found worthy to
be called unto the higher ministries in thy church,
through the same thy Son our Saviour Jesus Christ ;

to

to whom be glory and honour world without end. *Amen.*

PRevent us, O Lord, in all our doings with thy moſt gracious favour, and further us with thy continual help; that in all our works begun, continued, and ended in thee, we may glorify thy holy Name, and finally by thy mercy, obtain everlaſting life, through Jeſus Chriſt our Lord. *Amen.*

THE peace of God, which paſſeth all underſtanding, keep your hearts and minds in the knowledge and love of God, and of his Son Jeſus Chriſt our Lord. And the bleſſing of God Almighty, the Father, the Son, and the Holy Ghoſt, be amongſt you, and remain with you always. *Amen.*

The Form and Manner of ordaining of ELDERS.

When the Day appointed by the Superintendant is come, after Morning Prayer is ended, there ſhall be a Sermon or Exhortation, declaring the Duty and Office of ſuch as come to be admitted Elders; how neceſſary that Order is in the Church of Chriſt, and alſo how the People ought to eſteem them in their Office.

Firſt, one of the Elders ſhall preſent unto the Superintendant all them that are to be ordained, and ſay,

I Preſent unto you theſe perſons preſent, to be ordained Elders.

Then

*Then their Names being read aloud, the Superin-
tendant shall say unto the People;*

GOOD People, thefe are they whom we purpofe, God willing, this day to ordain Elders.
For after due examination, we find not to the contrary, but that they are lawfully called to this
function and miniftry, and that they are perfons
meet for the fame. But if there be any of you,
who knoweth any impediment or crime in any of
them, for the which he ought not to be received
into this holy miniftry, let him come forth in the
name of God, and fhew what the crime or impediment is.

*And if any Crime or Impediment be objected, the Super-
intendant shall surcease from ordaining that Person,
until such Time as the Party accused shall be found
clear of that Crime.*

*Then the Superintendant (commending such as shall be
found meet to be ordained, to the Prayers of the
Congregation) shall, with the Ministers and People
present, say the Litany, as is before appointed in the
Form of Ordaining Deacons, omitting the last
Prayer, and the Blessing.*

*Then shall be said the Service for the Communion;
with the Collect, Epistle, and Gospel, as followeth.*

The Collect.

ALmighty God, giver of all good things, who
by thy holy Spirit haft appointed divers orders
of minifters in thy church ; mercifully behold thefe
thy fervants now called to the office of Elders ;
and replenifh them fo with the truth of thy doctrine, and adorn them with innocency of life, that
both by word and good example they may faithfully ferve thee in this office, to the glory of thy
name, and the edification of thy church, through
the

the merits of our Saviour Jefus Chrift, who liveth and reigneth, with thee and the Holy Ghoft, world without end. *Amen.*

The Epiftle. Ephef. iv. 7.

UNto every one of us is given grace according to the meafure of the gift of Chrift. Wherefore he faith, When he afcended up on high, he led captivity captive, and gave gifts unto men. (Now that he afcended, what is it but that he alfo defcended firft into the lower parts of the earth? He that defcended, is the fame alfo that afcended up far above all things.) And he gave fome Apoftles, and fome prophets, and fome evangelifts, and fome paftors and teachers, for the perfecting of the faints, for the work of the miniftry, for the edifying of the body of Chrift; till we all come in the unity of the faith, and of the knowledge of the Son of God, unto a perfect man, unto the meafure of the ftature of the fulnefs of Chrift.

After this fhall be read for the Gofpel, part of the Tenth Chapter of Saint John.

S. *John,* x. 1.

VErily verily I fay unto you, He that entereth not by the door into the fheep-fold, but climbeth up fome other way, the fame is a thief and a robber. But he that entereth in by the door, is the fhepherd of the fheep. To him the porter openeth, and the fheep hear his voice; and he calleth his own fheep by name, and leadeth them out. And when he putteth forth his own fheep, he goeth before them, and the fheep follow him; for they know his voice. And a ftranger will they not follow, but flee from him; for they know not the voice of ftrangers. This parable fpake Jefus unto them, but they underftood not what things
they

they were which he fpake unto them. Then faid
Jefus unto them again, Verily verily I fay unto
you, I am the door of the fheep. All that ever
came before me are thieves and robbers; but the
fheep did not hear them. I am the door; by me
if any man enter in, he fhall be faved, and fhall
go in and out, and find pafture. The thief
cometh not but for to fteal, and to kill, and to
deftroy: I am come that they might have life, and
that they might have it more abundantly. I am
the good Shepherd: the good Shepherd giveth his
life for the fheep. But he that is an hireling, and
not the Shepherd, whofe own the fheep are not,
feeth the wolf coming, and leaveth the fheep, and
fleeth; and the wolf catcheth them, and fcattereth
the fheep. The hireling fleeth becaufe he is an
hireling, and careth not for the fheep. I am the
good Shepherd, and know my fheep, and am
known of mine. As the Father knoweth me,
even fo know I the Father: and I lay down my
life for the fheep. And other fheep I have, which
are not of this fold: them alfo I muft bring, and
they fhall hear my voice; and there fhall be one
fold, and one Shepherd.

*And that done, the Superintendant fhall fay unto them
as hereafter followeth,*

YOU have heard, brethren, as well in your private examination, as in the exhortation which
was now made to you, and in the holy leffons taken
out of the Gofpel, and the writings of the Apoftles,
of what dignity, and of how great importance this
office is, whereunto ye are called. And now
again we exhort you in the name of our Lord Jefus
Chrift, that you have in remembrance, into how
high a dignity, and to how weighty an office and
charge ye are called: That is to fay, to be Meffen-
gers, watchmen, and ftewards of the Lord; to
teach

teach, and to premonifh, to feed and provide for the Lord's family; to feek for Chrift's fheep that are difperfed abroad, and for his children who are in the midft of this naughty world, that they may be faved through Chrift for ever.

Have always therefore printed in your remembrance, how great a treafure is committed to your charge. For they are the fheep of Chrift, which he bought with his death, and for whom he fhed his blood. The church and congregation whom you muft ferve, is his Spoufe, and his body. And if it fhall happen, the fame church, or any member thereof do take any hurt or hindrance by reafon of your negligence, ye know the greatnefs of the fault, and alfo the horrible punifhment that will enfue. Wherefore confider with yourfelves the end of the miniftry towards the children of God, towards the fpoufe and body of Chrift; and fee that you never ceafe your labour, your care and diligence, until you have done all that lieth in you, according to your bounden duty, to bring all fuch as are or fhall be committed to your charge, unto that agreement in the faith and knowledge of God, and to that ripenefs and perfectnefs of age in Chrift, that there be no place left among you, either for error in religion, or for vicioufnefs in life.

Forafmuch then as your office is both of fo great excellency, and of fo great difficulty, ye fee with how great care and ftudy ye ought to apply yourfelves, as well that ye may fhew yourfelves dutiful and thankful unto that Lord, who hath placed you in fo high a dignity; as alfo to beware that neither you yourfelves offend, nor be occafion that others offend. Howbeit ye cannot have a mind and will thereto of yourfelves; for that will and ability is given of God alone: therefore ye ought, and have need to pray earneftly for his holy Spirit. And feeing that you cannot by any other means

N   compafs

compafs the doing of fo weighty a work, pertaining to the falvation of man, but with doctrine and
exhortation taken out of the Holy Scriptures, and
with a life agreeable to the fame: confider how
ftudious ye ought to be in reading and learning the
Scriptures, and in framing the manners both of
yourfelves, and of them that fpecially pertain unto
you, according to the rule of the fame Scriptures:
and for this felf-fame caufe, how ye ought to for-
fake and fet afide (as much as you may) all worldly
cares and ftudies.

We have good hope that you have all weighed
and pondered thefe things with yourfelves long
before this time; and that you have clearly determined, by God's grace, to give yourfelves wholly
to this office, whereunto it hath pleafed God to
call you: fo that, as much as lieth in you, you
will apply yourfelves wholly to this one thing, and
draw all your cares and ftudies this way, and that
you will continually pray to God the Father, by
the mediation of our only Saviour Jefus Chrift, for
the heavenly affiftance of the Holy Ghoft; that by
daily reading and weighing of the Scriptures, ye
may wax riper and ftronger in your miniftry; and
that ye may fo endeavour yourfelves from time to
time to fanctify the lives of you and your's, and to
fafhion them after the rule and doctrine of Chrift,
that ye may be wholefome and godly examples
and patterns for the people to follow.

And now that this prefent congregation of Chrift,
here affembled, may alfo underftand your minds
and wills in thefe things, and that this your promife may the more move you to do your duties; ye
fhall anfwer plainly to thefe things, which we, in
the Name of God, and of his Church, fhall demand of you touching the fame.

Do

DO you think in your heart, that you are truly called, according to the will of our Lord Jefus Chrift, to the order of Elders.

Anfwer. I think fo.

The Superintendant.

ARE you perfuaded that the Holy Scriptures contain fufficiently all doctrine required of neceffity for eternal falvation through faith in Jefus Chrift? And are you determined, out of the faid Scriptures to inftruct the people committed to your charge, and to teach nothing, as required of neceffity to eternal falvation, but that which you fhall be perfuaded, may be concluded and proved by the Scripture?

Anfwer. I am fo perfuaded, and have fo determined, by God's grace.

The Superintendant.

WILL you then give your faithful diligence, always fo to minifter the doctrine and facraments, and the difcipline of Chrift, as the Lord hath commanded.

Anfwer. I will fo do, by the help of the Lord.

The Superintendant.

WILL you be ready with all faithful diligence to banifh and drive away all erroneous and ftrange doctrines contrary to God's word; and to ufe both public and private monitions and exhortations, as well to the fick as to the whole within your diftrict, as need fhall require, and occafion fhall be given?

Anfwer. I will, the Lord being my helper.

The Superintendant.

WILL you be diligent in prayers, and in reading of the holy Scriptures, and in such studies as help to the knowledge of the same, laying aside the study of the world and the flesh.

Answer. I will endeavour so to do, the Lord being my helper.

The Superintendant.

WILL you be diligent to frame and fashion your own selves, and your families, according to the doctrine of Christ; and to make both yourselves and them, as much as in you lieth, wholesome examples and patterns to the flock of Christ?

Answer. I shall apply myself thereto, the Lord being my helper.

The Superintendant.

WILL you maintain and set forwards, as much as lieth in you, quietness, peace and love among all Christian people, and especially among them that are or shall be committed to your charge?

Answer. I will do so, the Lord being my helper.

The Superintendant.

WILL you reverently obey your chief ministers, unto whom is committed the charge and government over you; following with a glad mind and will their godly admonitions, and submitting yourselves to their godly judgments?

Answer. I will so do, the Lord being my helper.

Then shall the Superintendant standing up, say,

ALmighty God, who hath given you this will to do all these things; grant also unto you strength and power to perform the same; that he may

may accomplifh h's work which he hath begun in you, through Jefus Chrift our Lord. *Amen.*

After this the Congregation ſhall be deſired, ſecretly in their Prayers, to make their humb e Supplications to God for all theſe Things: for the which Prayers there ſhall be Silence kept for a Space.

*After which ſhall be ſaid by the Superintendant (the Perſons to be ordained Elders, all kneeling) V*eni, Creator, Spiritus; *the Superintendant beginning, and the Elders and others that are preſent anſwering by Verſes, as followeth.*

COme, Holy Ghoft, our ſouls inſpire,
 And lighten with celeſtial fire.
Thou the anointing Spirit art,
Who doſt thy ſev'nfold gifts impart :
Thy bleſſed Unction from above,
Is comfort, life, and fire of love.
Enable with perpetual light,
The dulneſs of our blinded ſight :
Anoint and cheer our foiled face
With the abundance of thy grace :
Keep far our foes, give peace at home;
Where thou art Guide no ill can come.
Teach us to know the Father, Son,
And thee of both, to be but one :
That through the ages all along,
This may be our endleſs Song;
Praiſe to thy eternal merit,
Father, Son, and Holy Spirit.

That done, the Superintendant ſhall pray in this wiſe, and ſay,

Let us pray.

ALmighty God, and heavenly Father, who of thine infinite love and goodneſs towards us, haſt given to us thy only and moſt dearly beloved

Son

Son Jefus Chrift to be our Redeemer, and the Author of everlafting life; who after he had made perfect our redemption by his death, and was afcended into heaven, fent abroad into the world his Apoftles, Prophets, Evangelifts, Doctors, and Paftors; by whofe labour and miniftry he gathered together a great flock in all the parts of the world, to fet forth the eternal praife of thy holy Name: for thefe fo great benefits of thy eternal goodnefs, and for that thou haft vouchfafed to call thefe thy fervants here prefent to the fame Office and Miniftry appointed for the falvation of mankind, we render unto thee moft hearty thanks, we praife and worfhip thee; and we humbly befeech thee by the fame thy bleffed Son, to grant unto all, who either here or elfewhere call upon thy holy Name, that we may continue to fhew ourfelves thankful unto thee for thefe and all other thy benefits; and that we may daily increafe and go forwards in the knowledge and faith of thee and thy Son by the Holy Spirit. So that as well by thefe thy Minifters, as by them over whom they fhall be appointed thy Minifters, thy holy Name may be for ever glorified, and thy bleffed kingdom enlarged, through the fame thy Son Jefus Chrift our Lord; who liveth and reigneth with thee in the unity of the fame Holy Spirit, world without end. *Amen.*

When this Prayer is done, the Superintendant, with the Elders prefent, fhall lay their hands feverally upon the Head of every one that receiveth the order of Elders: the Receivers humbly kneeling upon their knees, and the Superintendant faying,

REceive the Holy Ghoft for the Office and Work of an Elder in the Church of God, now committed unto thee by the impofition of our hands. And be thou a faithful Difpenfer of the Word of God, and of his holy Sacraments; in the Name of of the Father, and of the Son, and of the Holy Ghoſt. *Amen.*

Then the Superintendant ſhall deliver to every one of them, kneeling, the Bible into his hand, ſaying,

TAKE thou authority to preach the Word of God, and to adminiſter the holy Sacraments in the Congregation.

When this is done, the Superintendant ſhall go on in the Service of the Communion, which all they that receive Orders ſhall take together.

The Communion being done, after the laſt Collect, and immediately before the Benediction, ſhall be ſaid theſe Collects.

MOST merciful Father, we beſeech thee to ſend upon theſe thy ſervants thy heavenly bleſſing; that they may be clothed with righteouſneſs, and thy Word ſpoken by their mouths, may have ſuch ſucceſs, that it may never be ſpoken in vain. Grant alſo, that we may have grace to hear and receive what they ſhall deliver out of thy moſt holy Word, or agreeable to the ſame, as the means of our ſalvation; that in all our words and deeds we may ſeek thy glory, and the increaſe of thy kingdom, through Jeſus Chriſt our Lord. *Amen.*

PRevent us, O Lord, in all our doings, with thy moſt gracious favour, and further us with thy continual help; that in all our works begun, continued, and ended in thee, we may glorify thy holy Name, and finally by thy mercy obtain everlaſting life, through Jeſus Chriſt our Lord. *Amen.*

THE Peace of God, which paſſeth all underſtanding, keep your hearts and minds in the knowledge and love of God, and of his Son Jeſus Chriſt our Lord: and the bleſſing of God Almighty
the

the Father, the Son, and the Holy Ghoft, be amongft you, and remain with you always. *Amen.*

And if on the fame day the Order of Deacons be given to fome, and that of Elders to others; the Deacons fhall be firft prefented, and then the Elders; and it fhall fuffice, that the Litany be once faid for both. The Collects fhall both be ufed; firft, that for Deacons, then that for Elders. The Epiftle fhall be Ephef. iv. 7. *to* 13. *as before in this Office. Immediately after which, they that are to be ordained Deacons fhall be examined, and ordained, as is above prefcribed. Then one of them having read the Gofpel, which fhall be* St. John, x. 1. *as before in this Office; they that are to be ordained Elders, fhall likewife be examined and ordained, as is in this Office before appointed.*

The Form of Ordaining of a SUPERIN-TENDANT.

After Morning Prayer is ended, the Superintendant fhall begin the Communion Service; in which this fhall be

The Collect.

ALmighty God, who by thy Son Jefus Chrift didft give to thy holy Apoftles many excellent gifts, and didft charge them to feed thy flock; give grace, we befeech thee, to all the Minifters and Paftors of thy Church, that they may diligently preach thy Word, and duly adminifter the godly Difcipline thereof; and grant to the people, that they may obediently follow the fame; that all may receive the crown of everlafting glory, through Jefus Chrift our Lord. *Amen.*

Then

Then shall be read by one of the Elders, the Epistle.
Acts, xx. 17.

FROM Miletus Paul sent to Ephesus, and called the Elders of the Church. And when they were come to him, he said unto them, Ye know from the first day that I came into Asia, after what manner I have been with you at all seasons, serving the Lord with all humility of mind, and with many tears and temptations, which befel me by the lying in wait of the Jews : and how I kept back nothing that was profitable unto you, but have shewed you, and have taught you publickly, and from house to house, testifying both to the Jews, and also to the Greeks, repentance toward God, and faith toward our Lord Jesus Christ. And now behold, I go bound in the Spirit unto Jerusalem, not knowing the things that shall befal me there ; save that the Holy Ghost witnesseth in every city, saying, That bonds and afflictions abide me. But none of these things move me, neither count I my life dear unto myself, so that I might finish my course with joy, and the ministry which I have received of the Lord Jesus ; to testify the Gospel of the grace of God. And now, behold, I know that ye all, among whom I have gone preaching the Kingdom of God, shall see my face no more. Wherefore I take you to record this day, that I am pure from the blood of all men. For I have not shunned to declare unto you all the counsel of God. Take heed therefore unto yourselves, and to all the flock, over the which the Holy Ghost hath made you Overseers, to feed the Church of God, which he hath purchased with his own blood. For I know this, that after my departing shall grievous wolves enter in among you, not sparing the flock. Also of your own selves shall men arise, speaking perverse things, to draw away disciples after them.

N 5   Therefore

Therefore watch, and remember, that by the space of three years, I ceased not to warn every one night and day with tears. And now, brethren, I commend you to God, and to the word of his grace, which is able to build you up, and to give you an inheritance among them who are sanctified. I have coveted no man's silver, or gold, or apparel: yea, ye yourselves know, that these hands have ministered unto my necessities, and to them that were with me. I have shewed you all things, how that so labouring ye ought to support the weak; and to remember the words of the Lord Jesus, how he said, It is more blessed to give than to receive.

Then another Elder shall read,

The Gospel, St. John, xxi. 15.

JESUS saith to Simon Peter, Simon, son of Jonas lovest thou me more than these? He saith unto him, Yea, Lord; thou knowest that I love thee. He said unto him, Feed my lambs. He saith to him again the second time, Simon, son of Jonas, lovest thou me? He saith unto him, Yea, Lord; thou knowest that I love thee. He saith unto him, Feed my sheep. He saith unto him the third time, Simon, son of Jonas, lovest thou me? Peter was grieved because he said unto him the third time, Lovest thou me? And he said unto him, Lord, thou knowest all things: thou knowest that I love thee. Jesus saith unto him, Feed my sheep.

Or this: St. Matth. xxviii. 18.

JESUS came and spake unto them, saying, All power is given unto me in heaven and in earth. Go ye therefore and teach all nations, baptizing them, In the Name of the Father, and of the Son, and of the Holy Ghost; teaching them to observe
all

all things whatfoever I have commanded you; and lo, I am with you alway, even unto the end of the world.

After the Gofpel and the Sermon are ended, the elected Perfon fhall be prefented by two Elders unto the Superintendant, faying,

WE prefent unto you this godly Man to be ordained a Superintendant.

Then the Superintendant fhall move the Congregation prefent to pray, faying thus to them :

BRethren, it is written in the Gofpel of Saint Luke, That our Saviour Chrift continued the whole night in prayer, before he did choofe and fend forth his twelve Apoftles. It is written alfo in the Acts of the Apoftles, That the Difciples who were at Antioch, did faft and pray, before they laid hands on Paul and Barnabas, and fent them forth. Let us therefore, following the example of our Saviour Chrift, and his Apoftles, firft fall to Prayer before we admit, and fend forth this perfon prefented unto us, to the work, whereunto we truft the Holy Ghoft hath called him.

And then fhall be faid the Litany, as before, in the Form of Ordaining Deacons.

Then fhall be faid this Prayer following.

ALmighty God, giver of all good things, who by thy Holy Spirit haft appointed divers orders of minifters in thy church; mercifully behold this thy fervant now called to the work and miniftry of a Superintendant, and replenifh him fo with the truth of thy doctrine, and adorn him with innocency of life, that, both by word and deed, he may faithfully ferve thee in this office, to the glory of thy Name and the edifying and well-governing of thy church,

N 6

through the merits of our Saviour Jesus Christ, who liveth and reigneth with thee and the Holy Ghost, world without end. *Amen.*

Then the Superintendant shall say to him that is to be ordained,

BRother, forasmuch as the holy Scripture commands that we should not be hasty in laying on hands, and admitting any person to government in the church of Christ, which he hath purchased with no less price than the effusion of his own blood; before I admit you to this administration I will examine you on certain articles, to the end that the congregation present may have a trial, and bear witness how you are minded to behave yourself in the church of God.

ARE you persuaded that you are truly called to this ministration, according to the will of our Lord Jesus Christ?

Answer. I am so persuaded.

The Superintendant.

ARE you persuaded that the holy Scriptures contain sufficiently all doctrine required of necessity for eternal salvation, through faith in Jesus Christ? And are you determined out of the same holy Scriptures to instruct the people committed to your charge, and to teach or maintain nothing as required of necessity to eternal salvation, but that which you shall be persuaded may be concluded and proved by the same?

Answer. I am persuaded, and determined by God's grace.

The Superintendant.

WILL you then faithfully exercise yourself in the same holy Scriptures, and call upon God by prayer for the true understanding of the same,

so

fo as you may be able by them to teach and exhort with wholefome doctrine, and to withftand and convince the gainfayers ?

Anfwer. I will fo do, by the help of God.

The *Superintendant.*

ARE you ready, and with faithful diligence, to banifh and drive away all erroneous and ftrange doctrines contrary to God's Word, and both privately and openly to call upon and encourage others to the fame ?

Anfwer. I am ready, the Lord being my helper.

The *Superintendant.*

WILL you deny all ungodlinefs and worldly lufts, and live foberly, righteoufly, and godly in this prefent world, that you may fhew yourfelf in all things an example of good works unto others, that the adverfary may be afhamed, having nothing to fay againft you ?

Anfwer. I will fo do, the Lord being my helper.

The *Superintendant.*

WILL you maintain and fet forward, as much as fhall lie in you, quietnefs, love, and peace among all men ; and fuch as fhall be unquiet, difobedient, and criminal within your diftrict, correct and punifh, according to fuch authority as you have by God's Word, and as fhall be committed unto you.

Anfwer. I will fo do, by the help of God.

The *Superintendant.*

WILL you be faithful in ordaining, fending, or laying hands upon others ?

Anfwer. I will fo be, by the help of God.

The

The Superintendant.

WILL you shew yourself gentle, and be merciful, for Christ's sake, to poor and needy people, and to all strangers destitute of help?

Answer. I will so shew myself, by God's help.

Then the Superintendant shall say,

ALmighty God, our heavenly Father, who hath given you a good will to do all these things, grant also unto you strength and power to perform the same; that, he accomplishing in you the good work which he hath begun, you may be found perfect and irreprehensible at the last day, through Jesus Christ our Lord. *Amen.*

Then shall Veni Creator Spiritus *be said.*

COME, Holy Ghost, our souls inspire,
And lighten with celestial fire.
Thou the anointing Spirit art
Who dost thy sevenfold gifts impart :
Thy blessed unction from above
Is comfort, life, and fire of love.
Enable with perpetual light
The dulness of our blinded sight.
Anoint and cheer our soiled face
With the abundance of thy grace.
Keep far our foes, give peace at home :
Where thou art Guide no ill can come.
Teach us to know the Father, Son,
And thee of both, to be but one ;
That through the ages all along,
This may be our endless song,
Praise to thy eternal merit,
Father, Son, and Holy Spirit.

That

That ended, the Superintendant shall say,
Lord, hear our prayer.
Anf. And let our cry come unto thee.

Superintendant.
Let us pray.

ALmighty God and moft merciful Father, who of thine infinite goodnefs haft given thine only and dearly beloved Son Jefus Chrift to be our Redeemer, and the Author of everlafting life, who, after that he had made perfect our redemption by his death, and was afcended into heaven, poured down his gifts abundantly upon men, making fome Apoftles, fome Prophets, fome Evangelifts, fome Paftors and Doctors, to the edifying and making perfect his church; grant, we befeech thee, to this thy fervant fuch grace, that he may evermore be ready to fpread abroad thy gofpel, the glad tidings of reconciliation with thee, and ufe the authority given him, not to deftruction, but to falvation; not to hurt, but to help; fo that, as a wife and faithful fervant, giving to thy Family their portion in due feafon, he may at laft be received into everlafting joy, through Jefus Chrift our Lord, who, with thee and the Holy Ghoft, liveth and reigneth, One God, world without end. *Amen.*

Then the Superintendant and Elders prefent shall lay their Hands upon the Head of the elected Perfon kneeling before them upon his Knees, the Superintendant faying,

REceive the Holy Ghoft for the office and work of a Superintendant in the church of God, now committed unto thee by the impofition of our hands, in the Name of the Father, and of the Son,
and

and of the Holy Ghoſt. *Amen.* And remember that thou ſtir up the grace of God which is given thee by this impoſition of our hands ; for God hath not given us the ſpirit of fear, but of power, and love, and ſoberneſs.

Then the Superintendant ſhall deliver him the Bible, ſaying,

GIVE heed unto reading, exhortation, and doctrine. Think upon the things contained in this book. Be diligent in them, that the increaſe coming thereby may be manifeſt unto all men. Take heed unto thyſelf, and to thy doctrine ; for by ſo doing thou ſhalt both ſave thyſelf and them that hear thee. Be to the flock of Chriſt a ſhepherd, not a wolf ; feed them, devour them not. Hold up the weak, heal the ſick, bind up the broken, bring again the outcaſts, ſeek the loſt. Be ſo merciful, that you be not too remiſs ; ſo miniſter diſcipline that you forget not mercy ; that when the Chief Shepherd ſhall appear, you may receive the never-fading crown of glory, through Jeſus Chriſt our Lord. *Amen.*

Then the Superintendant ſhall proceed in the Communion Service , with whom the newly-ordained Superintendant, and other Perſons preſent, ſhall communicate.

And for the laſt Collect, immediately before the Benediction, ſhall be ſaid theſe Prayers.

MOST merciful Father, we beſeech thee to ſend down upon this thy ſervant thy heavenly bleſſing, and ſo endue him with thy Holy Spirit, that he, preaching thy word, may not only be earneſt to reprove, beſeech, and rebuke with all patience and doctrine, but alſo may be to ſuch as believe a wholeſome example in word, in converſa-

tion,

tion, in love, in faith, in chaftity, and in purity ; that faithfully fulfilling his courfe, at the latter day he may receive the crown of righteoufnefs laid up by the Lord, the righteous Judge, who liveth and reigneth one God with the Father and the Holy Ghoft, world without end. *Amen.*

PRevent us, O Lord, in all our doings with thy moft gracious favour, and further us with thy continual help, that in all our works begun, continued and ended in thee, we may glorify thy holy Name, and finally, by thy mercy, obtain everlafting life, through Jefus Chrift our Lord. *Amen.*

THE peace of God, which paffeth all underftanding, keep your hearts and minds in the knowledge and love of God, and of his Son Jefus Chrift our Lord ; and the bleffing of God Almighty the Father, the Son, and the Holy Ghoft, be amongft you, and remain with you always. *Amen.*

ARTICLES

ARTICLES of RELIGION.

I. *Of Faith in the Holy Trinity.*

THERE is but one living and true God, ever-lasting, without body, parts, or paffions; of infinite power, wifdom, and goodnefs; the Maker and Preferver of all things both vifible and invifible. And in unity of this Godhead there are three Per-fons of one fubftance, power, and eternity; the Father, the Son, and the Holy Ghoft.

II. *Of the Word, or Son of God, who was made very Man.*

THE Son, who is the Word of the Father, be-gotten from everlafting of the Father, the very and eternal God, of one fubftance with the Father, took man's nature in the womb of the bleffed Virgin: fo that two whole and perfect na-tures, that is to fay, the Godhead and Manhood, were joined together in one Perfon, never to be divided, whereof is one Chrift, very God, and very man, who truly fuffered, was crucified, dead, and buried, to reconcile his Father to us, and to be a facrifice, not only for original guilt, but alfo for actual fins of men.

III. *Of*

III. *Of the Resurrection of Christ.*

CHRIST did truly rise again from the dead, and took again his body, with all things appertaining to the Perfection of Man's Nature, wherewith he ascended into Heaven, and there sitteth until he return to judge all men at the last day.

IV. *Of the Holy Ghost.*

THE Holy Ghost, proceeding from the Father and the Son, is of one Substance, Majesty, and Glory, with the Father and the Son, very and eternal God.

V. *Of the Sufficiency of the Holy Scriptures for Salvation.*

HOLY Scripture containeth all things necessary to Salvation: so that whatsoever is not read therein, or may be proved thereby, is not to be required of any man, that it should be believed as an Article of the Faith, or be thought requisite or necessary to salvation. In the name of the Holy Scripture we do understand those Canonical Books of the Old and New Testament, of whose authority was never any doubt in the Church.

Of the Names of the Canonical Books.

GEnesis,
Exodus,
Leviticus,
Numbers,
Deuteronomy,
Joshua,
Judges,
Ruth,
The First Book of Samuel,
The Second Book of Samuel,

The

The Firſt Book of Kings,
The Second Book of Kings,
The Firſt Book of Chronicles,
The Second Book of Chronicles,
The Book of Ezra,
The Book of Nehemiah,
The Book of Heſter,
The Book of Job,
The Pſalms,
The Proverbs,
Ecclefiaſtes, or Preacher,
Cantica, or Songs of Solomon,
Four Prophets the greater,
Twelve Prophets the leſs.

All the Books of the New Teſtament, as they are commonly received, we do receive and account Canonical.

Of the Old Teſtament.

THE Old Teſtament is not contrary to the New; for both in the Old and New Teſtament ever-laſting life is offered to mankind by Chriſt, who is the only Mediator between God and Man, being both God and Man. Wherefore they are not to be heard, who feign that the old Fathers did look only for tranſitory promiſes Although the law given from God by Moſes, as touching Ceremo-nies and Rites, doth not bind Chriſtians, nor ought the Civil Precepts thereof of neceſſity to be received in any Commonwealth: yet notwith-ſtanding, no Chriſtian whatſoever is free from the obedience of the commandments which are called Moral.

VII. *Of*

VII. *Of Original or Birth-fin.*

ORiginal Sin ftandeth not in the following of Adam (as the Pelagians do vainly talk), but it is the corruption of the nature of every man, that naturally is ingendered of the offspring of Adam, whereby man is very far gone from original righteoufnefs, and of his own nature inclined to evil, and that continually.

VIII. *Of Free-will.*

THE condition of man after the fall of Adam is fuch that he cannot turn and prepare himfelf by his own natural ftren th·and works to faith, and calling upon God : Wherefore we have no power to do good works pleafant and acceptable to God, without the grace of God by Chrift preventing us, that we may have a good-will, and working with us, when we have that good-will.

IX. *Of the Juftification of Man.*

WE are accounted righteous before God, only for the merit of our Lord and Saviour Jefus Chrift, by faith, and not for our own works or defervings : wherefore, that we are juftified by faith only, is a moft wholefome doctrine, and very full of comfort.

X. *Of good Works.*

ALthough good Works, which are the fruits of Faith, and follow after Juftification, cannot put away our fins, and endure the feverity of God's judgment; yet are they pleafing and acceptable to God in Chrift, and fpring out of a true and lively Faith, infomuch that by them a lively Faith may be as evidently known, as a tree difcerned by its fruit.

XI. *Of*

XI. *Of Works of Supererogation.*

VOluntary Works, befides, over and above God's Commandments, which they call Works of Supererogation, cannot be taught without arrogancy and impiety. For by them men do declare, That they do not only render unto God as much as they are bound to do, but that they do more for his fake than of bounden duty is required : whereas Chrift faith plainly, When ye have done all that is commanded you, fay, We are unprofitable fervants.

XII. *Of Sin after Juftification.*

NOT every fin willingly committed after Jufti-fication, is the fin againft the Holy Ghoft, and unpardonable. Wherefore the grant of re-pentance is not to be denied to fuch as fall into fin, after juftification : after we have received the Holy Ghoft, we may depart from grace given, and fall into fin, and by the grace of God rife again, and amend our lives. And therefore they are to be condemned who fay they can no more fin as long as they live here, or deny the place of forgivenefs to fuch as truly repent.

XIII. *Of the Church.*

THE vifible Church of Chrift is a Congregation of faithful men, in the which the pure Word of God is preached, and the Sacraments duly ad-miniftered according to Chrift's Ordinance, in all thofe things that of neceffity are requifite to the fame.

XIV. *Of Purgatory.*

THE Romifh Doctrine concerning Purgatory, Pardons, Worfhipping, and Adoration, as well of Images, as of Reliques, and alfo Invoca-

tion

tion of Saints, is a fond thing vainly invented, and grounded upon no warrant of Scripture, but repugnant to the Word of God.

XV. *Of speaking in the Congregation in such a Tongue as the People understand.*

IT is a thing plainly repugnant to the Word of God, and the Custom of the Primitive Church, to have Publick Prayer in the Church, or to minister the Sacraments in a Tongue not understood by the People.

XVI. *Of the Sacraments.*

SAcraments ordained of Christ, are not only badges or tokens of Christian Men's Profession; but rather they are certain Signs of Grace, and God's good Will towards us, by the which he doth work invisibly in us, and doth not only quicken, but also strengthen and confirm our faith in him.

There are two Sacraments ordained of Christ our Lord in the Gospel; that is to say, Baptism, and the Supper of the Lord.

Those five commonly called Sacraments; that is to say, Confirmation, Penance, Orders, Matrimony, and extreme Unction, are not to be counted for Sacraments of the Gospel, being such as have grown, partly of the corrupt following of the Apostles, partly are states of life allowed in the Scriptures: but yet have not the like nature of Baptism and the Lord's Supper, because they have not any visible Sign or Ceremony ordained of God.

The sacraments were not ordained of Christ to be gazed upon, or to be carried about; but that we should duly use them. And in such only as worthily receive the same, they have a wholsome effect or operation: but they that receive them unworthily

thily

thily, purchafe to themfelves condemnation, as Saint *Paul* faith.

XVII. *Of Baptifm.*

BAptifm is not only a fign of profeffion, and mark of difference, whereby Chriftians are diftinguifhed from others that are not baptized; but it is alfo a fign of regeneration, or the new birth. The baptifm of young children is to be retained in the church.

XVIII. *Of the Lord's Supper.*

THE Supper of the Lord is not only a fign of the love that Chriftians ought to have among themfelves one to another, but rather is a facrament of our redemption by Chrift's death: Infomuch. that to fuch as rightly, worthily, and with faith receive the fame, the bread which we break is a partaking of the body of Chrift; and likewife the cup of bleffing is a partaking of the blood of Chrift.

Tranfubftantiation, or the change of the fubftance of bread and wine in the fupper of the Lord, cannot be proved by holy writ; but is repugnant to the plain words of Scripture, overthroweth the nature of a facrament, and hath given occafion to many fuperftitions.

The body of Chrift is given, taken, and eaten in the fupper, only after an heavenly and fpiritual manner. And the mean whereby the body of Chrift is received and eaten in the fupper, is faith.

The facrament of the Lord's fupper was not by Chrift's ordinance referved, carried about, lifted up, or worfhipped.

Of

XIX. *Of both Kinds.*

THE cup of the Lord is not to be denied to the lay-people; for both the parts of the Lord's Supper, by Chrift's ordinance and commandment, ought to be miniftered to all Chriftians alike.

XX. *Of the One Oblation of Chrift, finifhed upon the Crofs.*

THE offering of Chrift once made, is that per- fect redemption, propitiation, and fatisfaction for all the fins of the whole world, both original and actual; and there is none other fatisfaction for fin but that alone. Wherefore the facrifice of maffes, in the which it is commonly faid that the prieft doth offer Chrift for the quick and the dead, to have remiffion of pain or guilt, is a blafphemous fable, and dangerous decei.

XXI. *Of the Marriage of Minifters.*

THE minifters of Chrift are not commanded by God's law either to vow the eftate of fingle life, or to abftain from marriage; therefore it is lawful for them, as for all other Chriftians, to marry at their own difcretion, as they fhall judge the fame to ferve beft to godlinefs.

XXII. *Of the Rites and Ceremonies of Churches.*

IT is not neceffary that rites and ceremonies fhould in all places be the fame, or exactly alike; for they have been always different, and may be changed according to the diverfity of coun- tries, times, and men's manners, fo that nothing be ordained againft God's word. Whofoever, through his private judgment, willingly and pur- pofely doth openly break the rites and ceremonies

O

of

of the church to which he belongs, which are not repugnant to the word of God, and are ordained and approved by common authority, ought to be rebuked openly, that others may fear to do the like, as one that offendeth against the common order of the church, and woundeth the consciences of weak brethren.

Every particular church may ordain, change, or abolish rites and ceremonies, so that all things may be done to edification.

XXIII. *Of Christian Men's Goods.*

THE riches and goods of Christians are not common as touching the right, title, and possession of the same, as some do falsely boast. Notwithstanding, every man ought, of such things as he possesseth, liberally to give alms to the poor according to his ability.

XXIV. *Of a Christian Man's Oath.*

AS we confess that vain and rash swearing is forbidden Christian men by our Lord Jesus Christ, and *James* his apostle; so we judge that the Christian religion doth not prohibit, but that a man may swear when the magistrate requireth, in a cause of faith and charity, so it be done according to the Prophet's teaching, in justice, judgment, and truth.

F I N I S.

brought out of darknefs and error, into the clear light and true knowledge of thee, and of thy Son Jefus Chrift. Therefore with Angels, &c.

Upon the Feaft of Trinity.

WHO art one God, one Lord ; not one only perfon, but three perfons in one fubftance. For that which we believe of the glory of the Father, the fame we believe of the Son, and of the Holy Ghoft, without any difference or inequality. Therefore with Angels, &c.

After each of which Prefaces fhall immediately be faid,

THerefore with Angels and Archangels, and with all the company of heaven, we laud and magnify thy glorious Name, evermore praifing thee, and faying, Holy, holy, holy, Lord God of hofts, heaven and earth are full of thy glory. Glory be to thee, O Lord moft high. Amen.

Then fhall the Elder, kneeling down at the Table, fay, in the Name of all them that fhall receive the Communion, this Prayer following ; the People alfo kneeling :

WE do not prefume to come to this thy Table, O merciful Lord, trufting in our own righteoufnefs, but in thy manifold and great mercies. We are not worthy fo much as to gather up the crumbs under thy table. But thou art the fame Lord, whofe property is always to have mercy : Grant us therefore, gracious Lord, fo to eat the flefh of thy dear Son Jefus Chrift, and to drink his blood, that our finful bodies may be made clean by his body, and our fouls wafhed through his moft precious blood, and that we may evermore dwell in him, and he in us. *Amen.*

Then

Then the Elder shall say the Prayer of Consecration, as followeth:

ALmighty God, our heavenly Father, who, of thy tender mercy, didst give thine only Son Jesus Christ to suffer death upon the cross for our redemption; who made there (by his oblation of himself once offered) a full, perfect, and sufficient sacrifice, oblation, and satisfaction for the sins of the whole world; and did institute, and in his holy Gospel command us to continue, a perpetual memory of that his precious death until his coming again; hear us, O merciful Father, we most humbly beseech thee, and grant that we, receiving these thy creatures of bread and wine, according to thy Son our Saviour Jesus Christ's holy institution, in remembrance of his death and passion, may be partakers of his most blessed Body and Blood: who, in the same night that he was betrayed, took bread; and when he had given thanks, he brake it, and gave it to his disciples, saying, Take, eat; this is my Body which is given for you: Do this in remembrance of me. Likewise, after supper, he took the cup; and when he had given thanks, he gave it to them, saying, Drink ye all of this; for this is my blood of the New Testament, which is shed for you, and for many, for the remission of sins: Do this, as oft as ye shall drink it, in remembrance of me. *Amen.*

Then shall the Minister first receive the Communion in both kinds himself, and then proceed to deliver the same to the other Ministers in like manner, (if any be present) and after that to the People also, in order, into their Hands. And when he delivereth the Bread to any one, he shall say,

THE Body of our Lord Jesus Christ, which was given for thee, preserve thy body and soul unto everlasting life. Take and eat this in remem-

I

brance

not enter therein. And he took them up in his arms, put his hands upon them, and bleffed them.

Then fholl the Minifter fay,

ALmighty and everlafting God, heavenly Father, we give thee humble thanks that thou haft vouchfafed to call us to the knowledge of thy grace and faith in thee, increafe this knowledge, and confirm this faith in us evermore. Give thy Holy Spirit to *this Infant*, that *he* may be born again, and be made *an heir* of everlafting falvation, through our Lord Jefus Chrift, who liveth and reigneth with thee and the Holy Spirit, now and for ever. *Amen.*

O Merciful God, grant that the old Adam in *this Child* may be fo buried, that the new man may be raifed up in *him*. *Amen.*

Grant that all carnal affections may die in *him*, and that all things belonging to the Spirit may live and grow in *him*. *Amen.*

Grant that *he* may have power and ftrength to have victory, and to triumph againft the devil, the world, and the flefh. *Amen.*

Grant that whofoever is dedicated to thee by our office and miniftry, may alfo be endued with heavenly virtues, and everlaftingly rewarded, through thy mercy, O bleffed Lord God, who doft live and govern all things, world without end. *Amen.*

ALmighty everliving God, whofe moft dearly beloved Son Jefus Chrift, for the forgivenefs of our fins, did fhed out of his moft precious fide both water and blood, and gave commandment to his difciples that they fhould go teach all nations, and baptize them in the Name of the Father, and of the Son, and of the Holy Ghoft, regard, we be-

feech

feech thee, the fupplications of thy congregation ; fanctify this water to the myftical wafhing away of fin ; and grant that *this Child*, now to be baptized, may receive the fulnefs of thy grace, and ever remain in the number of thy faithful and elect children, through Jefus Chrift our Lord. *Amen.*

Then the Minifter fhall take the Child into his Hands, and fay to the Friends of the Child,
Name this Child.

And then, naming it after them, he fhall dip it in the Water, or fprinkle it therewith, faying,

N. I baptize thee, in the Name of the Father, and of the Son, and of the Holy Ghoft, *Amen.*

Then fhall the Minifter fay,

SEeing now, dearly beloved brethren, that *this Child is* grafted into the body of Chrift's Church, let us give thanks unto Almighty God for thefe benefits, and with one accord make our prayers unto him, that *this Child* may lead the reft of *his life* according to this beginning.

Then fhall be faid, all kneeling,

OUR Father who art in heaven, Hallowed be thy Name ; Thy kingdom come ; Thy will be done on earth, as it is in heaven : Give us this day our daily bread ; And forgive us our trefpaffes, as we forgive them that trefpafs againft us : And lead us not into temptation ; But deliver us from evil. *Amen.*

Then fhall the Minifter fay,

WE yield thee hearty thanks, moft merciful Father, that it hath pleafed thee to receive *this Infant* for thine own *Child* by adoption, and to incorporate *him* into thy holy Church. And humbly

bly we befeech thee to grant, that *he,* being dead unto fin, and living unto righteoufnefs, and being buried with Chrift in his death, may crucify the old man, and utterly abolifh the whole body of fin; and that, as *he is* made *partaker* of the death of thy Son, *he* may alfo be *partaker* of his refurrection ; fo that finally, with the refidue of thy holy Church, *he* may be *an inheritor* of thine everlafting kingdom, through Chrift our Lord. *Amen.*

The Miniftration of BAPTISM to fuch as are of RIPER YEARS.

The Minifter fhall fay,

DEarly beloved, forafmuch as all men are conceived and born in fin (and that which is born of the flefh is flefh, and they that are in the flefh cannot pleafe God, but live in fin, committing many actual tranfgreffions) ; and that our Saviour Chrift faith, None can enter into the kingdom of God, except he be regenerate and born anew of water and of the Holy Ghoft; I befeech you to call upon God the Father, through our Lord Jefus Chrift, that of his bounteous goodnefs he will grant to *thefe Perfons,* that which by nature *they* cannot have; that *they* may be baptized with Water and the Hòly Ghoft, and received into Chrift's holy Church, and be made lively *members* of the fame.

Then fhall the Minifter fay,

Let us pray. .

(And here all the Congregation fhall kneel.)

ALmighty and everlafting God, who of thy great mercy didft fave Noah and his family in the ark from perifhing by water; and alfo didft

fafely

safely lead the children of Ifrael thy people through the Red Sea, figuring thereby thy holy Baptifm; and by the Baptifm of thy well-beloved Son Jefus Chrift in the river Jordan, didft fanctify the element of water to the myftical wafhing away of fin; We befeech thee, for thine infinite mercies, that thou wilt mercifully look upon *thefe* thy *Servants*; wafh *them* and fanctify *them* with the Holy Ghoft; that *they* being delivered from thy wrath, may be received into the ark of Chrift's Church; and being ftedfaft in faith, joyful through hope, and rooted in charity, may fo pafs the waves of this troublefome world, that finally *they* may come to the land of everlafting life; there to reign with thee, world without end, through Jefus Chrift our Lord. *Amen.*

ALmighty and immortal God, the aid of all that need, the helper of all that flee to thee for fuccour, the life of them that believe, and the refurrection of the dead; We call upon thee for *thefe Perfons*; that *they* coming to thy holy Baptifm, may receive remiffion of *their* fins by fpiritual regeneration. Receive *them*, O Lord, as thou haft promifed by thy well-beloved Son, faying, Afk, and ye fhall receive; feek, and ye fhall find; knock, and it fhall be opened unto you: So give now unto us that afk; let us that feek find; open the gate unto us that knock; that *thefe Perfons* may enjoy the everlafting benediction of thy heavenly wafhing, and may come to the eternal kingdom which thou haft promifed by Chrift our Lord. *Amen.*

Then